CROSS MARKETING MAGIC

FOR AUTHORS

Developing New Avenues

for Advanced Book Marketing

by

Deborah Riley-Magnus

Published by Little Pen Press

Copyright © 2013 Deborah Riley-Magnus
All rights reserved.

ISBN-10: 1543203264
ISBN-13: 978-1-54320-326-4

DEDICATION

To the magic of creativity,
and authors who fight dragons for exceptional marketing success.

CONTENTS

INTRODUCTION

There's magic everywhere! It's in the whispers of the muse, in the changing seasons, and in life all around us. Magic plays with our imagination and spurs us on to do better and greater things. I first discovered magic when I was a child and watched Disney's Fantasia for the first time. The film was released in 1940, and having been born more than a decade later, I never got to see it on the silver screen. But when I did witness the magic and craft of this film on television, something snapped inside my mind and changed my view of the world forever. I was just a little girl, and that movie brought more than just fantastical dancing hippos and mystical sweeps of a spelled broom. It made me wonder at the magic of imagination, the power of an artist's skills and the remarkable entertainment garnered from such delightful approaches to the mundane world.

I believe that authors instinctively know that magic is in every nuance of our lives. As creative thinkers and problem solvers, authors seek inspiration every moment of the day and night. We pull ideas from dreams and snippets of conversation and we extrapolate those visions into stories meant to entice, titillate, and surprise readers. Authors seek magic in the ability to hone our craft and bring more readers to our books. We look for the magic of words and the mystical, hypnotic, rhythmic music they create. We know that there are numinous elements at play when we pitch our books to literary agents and/or publishers. We seek the mysterious avenues where we can gain recognition and build a reputation as a good writer, and we struggle to perfect the enchantment of marketing, whether we've found traditional publishing or chosen to self-publish, whether we write genre novels, experimental fiction, or nonfiction.

We take classes and workshops, read books, and listen to successful authors in hopes of capturing the magic they've already found and mastered. We writers are a determined sort and we want every charmed trick we can find to be successful at it.

My first nonfiction book, *Finding Author Success: Discovering and Uncovering the Marketing Power within your Manuscript,* was written to help writers and authors understand the basics of marketing. It covered why we need to use it, how to set up our platforms to bring the market to us, and the best ways to make our unique books stand apart from the crowd. It's estimated that more than a thousand new books are released every day. Between traditional publishers, mid-sized publishers, small publishers, and self-publishing authors, the deluge is massive. Perfecting and using powerful strategies to be heard over the din is vital. *Finding Author Success* helped many authors find their way and become successful. So, why do we need another book?

Cross Marketing Magic for Authors: Developing New Avenues for Advanced Book Marketing is a timely collection of highly effective, sophisticated strategies for authors ready to push beyond the reach of basic marketing. Fundamental marketing still runs the magic show because as in anything from sports to business to baking cookies, without the basics, everything falls apart. This book is designed to help authors revive sales that have flat lined, increase backlist sales, and catapult new books into different and lucrative realms of targeted marketing. In these pages the author will be asked to dig deeper into their manuscript, whether fiction or nonfiction, to find new market targets that have previously been undiscovered. They're there, I promise you. It just takes some serious excavating and a touch of magic to find them. It's time to become marketing wizards! Grab your wands and let's get started.

PART 1
REVIEWING THE BASICS

"Electricity is just really organized lightning."

~ George Carlin

No matter what a person does, mastering the basics is the key to success. A struggling baseball team goes back to the basics for fielding, pitching, and skills improvement by practicing, practicing, practicing. The basics for chemistry, physics, and baking a cake are finite and must be adhered to, or no one gets dessert. We all pay attention to basic good manners, basic appropriate fashion, and basic logic. The basics are everywhere, from grammar school etiquette to job interview skills, and without mastering them we can't build something bigger and better.

Before we move on to the enchantment and charms of developing new avenues for advanced book marketing, we will cover what I feel are the most important basics for author marketing, promotions, and publicity. Strangely, these basics work no matter what your product might be, whether you run a haberdashery or an art gallery. Whether your company builds computer chips or produces rock and roll hits. In all cases, you will pitch your idea or product, create platforms for exposing it, develop marketing to create awareness for it, deal with the media to publicize it, and work your creative muscles to actively promote the sale of it. After all, even wizards need to practice and master the basics.

START WITH A GREAT BOOK BUSINESS PLAN

Since we're reviewing the basics, I wanted to start here. Writers   write.

Successful authors write a book business plan. I know no one likes to hear this, even my clients who are not of the author persuasion, but without a business plan you are going nowhere.

It's vital for a writer to have a book business plan because your books and you are the products to be sold. It makes most writers queasy to even imagine selling themselves but without a plan, you can hardly figure out a way for your book to sell itself. Think of it as a map designed to take you from starving writer to successful author.

Since I'm talking to writers, I've decided to take this nice and easy, no sudden movements or anything like that. Let's start with a simple comparison. If you want to write a book, what do you need? Don't say nothing but your imagination because we both know that's not so. You need a slamming idea and you need some talent. Some writers begin the process with paper and pen. If you're not a pencil kind of writer, you've got a computer. Now, we're not covering writer's block or terminal confusion here, so let's assume you now have your tools of preference and are ready to scratch out the next great novel. We all know what comes next.

Some writers work organically and let the story tell itself, some like outlines. Some prefer pretty, colorful mind maps, charts, or graphs. In any case, you're on the road to understanding the book business plan process.

After the story is written, you edit, you get other people to read your work, you edit again, and you begin the process of finding publication. We're not exploring agents or publishing methods today. Any writer can write a book – good, bad or mediocre – but only a smart author knows that they also need to write a business plan, because only a successful author knows that they are now in business.

At what point do you start your book business plan? I'm going to toss this out, so duck if you're too afraid to catch, but the book business plan starts when the book starts. This plan covers all aspects of the product. At the moment you begin a novel or nonfiction book, you must already have a clear vision of the message, the audience, and even the venues and arenas where it can be sold. This isn't wishful thinking. This is the beginning of your plan.

My strongest suggestion is to ask the business plan developer (that's you) to start at the end. Start with your end goal. Don't be ridiculous and say you intend to be the next number one best seller worldwide and you want it now. Of course, you can be the number one best seller eventually. Just remember, number one best sellers had to go through this process, so you'll have to pay your dues too.

Nonfiction writers will have a far better grasp on this than fiction writers for one simple reason: nonfiction writers are required to develop a proposal before they even start writing. If fiction writers took on the same project, they'd have a far better chance at sales success. A friend once told me, "I'd rather stick to the fantasy than write the facts of selling it." The problem is that you can't have success without both. So, realize that when you start writing your book, you also should start writing your book business plan. If your book is finished and even published and out there in the world, it's not too late, so no excuses.

How do you write a book business plan? Imagine you're sitting at the bank, talking across the desk to the loan manager and asking for money. What's he going to ask you? Those are the questions you need to answer when putting together your book business plan.

- **How much money to you want?** This should be an easy answer. How successful do you want to be? Think of the imaginary loan amount as the financial success you want to gain from your book sales. Be realistic, you most likely won't make millions with your first novel, but if you set the right strategy, you could make millions down the road with your fifth, sixth, or tenth book.

- **How do you plan to organize and manage your product?** Yes, they do ask that and you should have an answer when your imaginary loan officer spits out those words. Exactly what is your plan for dealing with the organization and management of your new book? Should you have a publicist? Do you need an advertising agency? A book video? Imprinted bookmarks or T-shirts? Remember to research everything and be sure of the success rate for each element you want to employ. It's a lot to think about. Can you do it alone? Managing the product means clearly understanding it. So now is a good time to face the fact that you are the product as much as your book. Your creativity, your talent as a writer, your expertise, your personality, your skills, and your book.

- **Who will want to buy your product?** Now is the time to jot down all those people who will want your book, why they'll want it, and how effective they'll be at getting more people to want it. Really know who your market and readership target is. Are they men? Women? Knowing your target reader is as important as knowing good spelling and grammar. It will determine the venues you choose when the book is ready to be sold.

- **What makes your product so special?** You better know this or step away from the keyboard right now. No point in writing a book if you don't know why or whether it's special or not. Many writers write books they'd love to read, many write books readers are buying, some write books because the subject is risky or has never been explored before. Know why you and your book are special. It's the backbone of a successful book business plan.

- **How do you plan to promote your product?** This is where most writers cower in a corner. Relax. You know people, lots of people. And those people know people. You must put yourself out there. Of course there are the big things you must do: social networking, book events, gaining reviews and interviews, speaking engagements, attending workshops and panels, but don't forget your friends. Most writers have or have had another life, another career, or another circle of activity that has made their lives full. Don't forget your friends, work associates, and family. Let old buddies from college or work know that you have a book out there. You may be surprised the buzz that can be generated when you post your book one-sheet on the dentist or vet office's cork board. People like to support people they know. This is a powerful, easy tool to enhance the big stuff mentioned earlier.

- **What are your marketing strategies?** Think about it. Yes, it's cool to have your book available on Amazon or in your local book store, but where else might it fit in perfectly? Stretch your mind and think this through. If your novel is about travel, maybe you should seek distribution at a travel agency or on travel agency websites. If the story revolves around people drinking coffee, coffee shops often sell gift items and books. Is the story about wine? Wineries have wonderful gift shops. If your novel is historic in nature, perhaps museum gift stores can be a venue. Be creative. After all, that's what writers do, think creatively.

- **What if you fail?** Forget it. I have a very strong theory that failure is just the lack of seeking success. When someone tells you that you can't do something or market a book that way, do it anyway. Chances are it just hasn't been tried or it hasn't proven effective for someone less aggressive or creative. There's a slogan I use with my clients, "We are the can-do team." Go on, tell me I can't and guess what, I do. So can you.

Now you have a book business plan. It maps out who you want to sell your book to and how successful you want to be with it. See, that didn't hurt one bit, did it? All you need to do now is follow the plan. Let it grow and fluctuate but always keep your eye on the prize. Ebb and flow in a good plan is a good thing, as long as the end goal is always at the top of your mind. Who knows, you may even exceed your expectations, but how will you ever know if you haven't set the goals in the first place?

Just like working on your book, show your business plan to people, let them make suggestions and offer ideas. Share what you've learned with other authors and again you will find your sphere of influence expanding. Everything about the process is good and positive.

And it's the best place to use the basics of good planning.

THE PERFECT 25 WORD PITCH

"Nine out of ten dentists recommend Crest toothpaste over any other leading whitening toothpaste on the market today."

– Proctor and Gamble Company

"With knowledgeable investment guidance, advanced trading tools, and an extensive library of educational resources – investing has never been easier."

– TD Ameritrade On-line Investing Company

Perdue Farms is dedicated to enhancing the quality of life for everyone we touch through innovative food and agricultural products – *Perdue Foods Company.*

What you've just read is 25 – 30 words of power from three different industries. If you look around, you'll find these tiny pitches everywhere, and they serve a major purpose. They get the point of their product across in a way that makes it not only stand apart, but tells the benefits of the product or service as well.

How does this apply to authors? Why do you need a 25 word pitch about your book or series of books? Of course there's the obvious, to pitch your book to literary agents or publishers. But even if you've chosen to pass on a literary agent or publisher and decide to self-publish, you still need a strong 25 word pitch. We writers query for a lot of things aside from agent or publisher consideration. We query for book reviews, for speaking engagements, book signing events, and when we offer to do readings. A press release is a query, asking the media to write a story about us and our book. We query charities when we want to create or participate in a supportive event related to our book subject. In other words, authors query all the time. It's best to have the perfectly crafted 25 –30 word pitch in your pocket to make sure your queries have the most polished impact possible. After all, you never know when someone who can change your life will come along and ask, "What's your book about?"

With the perfect 25 word pitch, an author will have a leg up at getting what they want. The trick to crafting the perfect 25 – 30 word pitch is to follow three simple points. Your pitch must convey:

- Who will relate to your book? (The target demographic)
- The genre of your book? (If nonfiction, the specific subject and reader interest)
- What is your book about?

Your pitch must get all this across without using words like urban fantasy or mystery, without saying "women will love this story", and without telling too much or too little about your story. It can't be over 30 words and it can't read like a laundry list. Remember, when someone reads or asks to hear what your book is about, they also expect to read or hear something as well written as the book.

Here are few examples of great pitches I've heard over the years and why they work so well. These are random pitches from various students in many different workshops I've taught, but they've stuck with me because they are the perfect 25 word pitches for those books.

- An anarchist punk faery with mob ties takes on one last job with the help of a vengeful shape-shifting slave soldier in 1979 Philadelphia.
  - This one is wonderful. It covers all the bases. I understand that women and young adults will love this book. The words faery and 1979 Philadelphia tell me that it's an urban fantasy. The story is clearly outlined, as far as conveying that there's a cool edginess and terrific sense of humor in the book. The pitch flows smoothly off the tongue and tells me the writer writes very well.
- When a socially phobic woman reconnects with the world to rescue her mother from financial ruin, the last thing she expects to find is true love.
  - The target demographic for this book is women, probably 25 to 50. The genre is contemporary romance and the way the author related the story, I already have sympathy for the main

character. It's well written and reads smoothly.

- Desperate to escape her tortured past, a teenage genius learns she has multiple personality disorder when she is arrested for the kidnap and murder of her four-year-old half sister.
    - WOW, every time I read this one I love it more. The target reader is young adults and women over 50 (mainly because more women over 50 read YA than young adults – good thing to know when marketing a YA). The genre is contemporary young women's fiction and the story kicks butt. This author didn't hold back anything when they wrote this powerful pitch.
- Every American must separate economics from politics to vote responsibly. In straightforward terms, this book offers undeniable proof of our country's destiny and how you can change its course.
    - The target reader for this book is Americans, men, women, and young adults of voting age. This is nonfiction, and the message is put forth without the least bit of sugar coating. The pitch is perfect for the subject matter.

Developing your perfect pitch is only part of the task here. You also need to use it every chance you get. It's the perfect Facebook post, the perfect introduction kick for when you are speaking, doing a reading or a book signing. It's part of your promotions, the punch in your query requests, press releases and emails. It's the perfect email tag line. This is the perfect answer for when anyone asks, "So, what's your book about?" You should have your 25 word pitch memorized so that it rolls off your tongue with ease and elegance.

And you should know how to take that 25 word pitch down to a 10 – 15 word sound bite. A 10 word sound bite is the perfect tweet, that kicky open when you launch into your speech or before you do your reading. It's the hook of your 25 word pitch, and when you have your pitch and your sound bite perfected, it's a golden double-barreled blast.

To help you write your 10 – 15 word sound bite, all you need to do is focus on the core of your 25 word pitch. In your sound bite, you still need to get all the information across. The easiest trick I know for guiding you is to suggest that you write a 10 – 15 word sound bite for one of your favorite books by another author. You'll be amazed how easy it is. After you've done a few of those, launch into your own. The perfect sound bite is great on everything from promotions to promotional items. It can be the perfect title line on your website or that cool description on your blog.

Writing these pitches and sound bites is a practice in being succinct and tight, but also an opportunity to show your word muscle as a writer. Armed with both a great 25 word pitch and 10 word sound bite, you are half way home for all your promotion and marketing.

PLATFORM BUILDING

Everyone has heard about platforms, and every author has a slightly different idea of how they work. Usually I explain platforms development and function from the author out, but this time I thought I'd go the other way – from the fan or information seeker, in.

Author Platform Website

Let's imagine you're a journalist and you write for a publication. Your assignment is to locate and interview romance authors who have written three or more books. You are to write a story about each of them for your highly read magazine and uncover the inspiration that drives romance writers.

Now, how will you find these romance authors? As a reporter, the last thing you care to do is Google romance writers then slosh your way through all the many colorful, dynamic, interactive websites with instant music playing in the background that attract the author's fans. You want information and you want it easily. Otherwise, you simply cross that author off your list and move on to the next. You're a very busy person.

This is where the author platform venue comes into play. So many authors balk at the idea of having a separate author platform website because they think it's too time consuming and unimportant, but when that journalist comes calling, an author feels very differently about it. An author platform website could be a simple website or a blog format that includes a few tabs. This website is so clean and simple and easy to navigate even a monkey could get around, so any busy journalist can use it without difficulty or distraction. Avoid fancy images and colorful creativity here. Keep it simple, professional and clean. Think of this author platform website as your business office.

Four simple things go in your author platform website.

- **Introduction/Home Page** – Bio, your photo, some background, but keep it simple.
- **Book(s) Page** – Again, keep this simple. The cover art, brief 25 word

pitch/synopsis, and a buy link for each book is all you need here. Then link each book to your book platform website so that the viewer could see more if they want to.

- **Activities Page** – It's vital to keep this one updated regularly. This page lists your speaking engagements, release dates, launch events or dates, and locations of your book signings. This page can list some of your sterling reviews, a collection of podcast interview links, or videos of your activities.

- **Media Room** – This one is super important, it's what the reporter or journalist is looking for. You will include everything the media could want and make it as simple as possible for them to access it. You also need to put contact information on this page, either your email address or the phone number of the contact or publicist who will arrange for further information the media may request. In your media room you need the following items. Make sure everything is downloadable, *and check those often.* There's nothing uglier than a media person complaining that they couldn't download something they wanted. They get irritated and the last thing we want to do is irritate the media.
  - Author photo, current and nice. It's not necessary for it to be professionally done but please make sure you look professional.
  - Author bio, this is a full bio with education, accomplishments, memberships, awards, association affiliations, and special interests. Many interviewers in the media pick up some piece of interest from those kinds of bios and like to use them for casual approaches to the author. For example: *The author lives in her Chicago apartment with her husband, teenage son, and three English bulldogs.* You need to keep this bio up to date, so check it often.
  - Jpeg of your book cover(s).
  - Brief synopsis of the book(s).
  - Copies of all the press releases you've sent out.
  - All contact information.

NOTE: All the items in your media room should also be in your hands as hard copies so that should you come across a contact who doesn't wish to download the items, you can easily snail mail them a packet.

Book Platform Website

Okay, now let's imagine you're an avid reader and big fan of mystery novels. You Google your favorite author to find their book platform website and it's a treasure trove of entertainment and exploration. The website is exciting and colorful, plays with the various themes within the author's books and holds your interest. It changes and updates often, so you're sure to favorite that website and go there often.

Now, let's just imagine that you love reading cozy mysteries, those light but interesting mysteries that always come out well and make you feel good. You begin to explore all the various book platform websites and you stumble on to one that looks like you might really love. The book descriptions are exactly what you're looking for and the covers are interesting. The reviews are great so you are pretty happy, until you explore further and discover an entire section of the website dedicated to hard erotica short stories and novels.

The author has lost this prospective fan and book buyer for ever. Why? Not because that author didn't write the perfect books for the reader. Not because the website wasn't interesting and creative. The author lost this prospective fan and book buyer because they didn't understand the first rule of marketing. Always know and respect your audience.

By combining both their hot erotica and cozy mysteries on one website, they might have saved some time and energy for themselves, but they did not respect their audience. Whenever an author writes in two distinctly different genres – it doesn't have to be as drastic as cozy mystery and erotica, or children's books and dark horror, it could be as simple as the author writing fiction and nonfiction, or romance and science fiction – it's vital to focus on each audience separately. People who love science fiction are a breed unto themselves, and trying to mix them into the same space with people who read historic memoirs is foolish. Even the big brick and mortar book stores know better. That's why everything is sectioned and separated out.

Book platform websites should always honor the fan and prospective book buyer. This DOES NOT mean that you need a separate book platform website for each book by any means. If you write romance, there's no reason you can't have contemporary romance, historical romance, paranormal romance, humorous romance, and even YA romance on the same website. Readers will never be offended or confused because they are looking for romance. They can explore all through the website and discover all your talent. NOW, I'm sure I don't need to explain that putting YA romance and erotic romance on the same website is a no-no. Always use common sense. If I want to read women's fiction, I don't care to field through nonfiction books about green living or how to fix my garbage disposal. I want to find the genre I want to buy and read.

When designing your website, imagine walking through a department store. You would find lingerie in Macy's, but you're not likely to find sex toys there. You will find denim jeans for every age and size, but not workman's overalls and shoes for mining, or uniforms for chefs. Remembering that your fan and prospective book buyer is very important to your future, isn't it worth it to consider separating out some of your books? I promise, if your nonfiction or hard erotica are on separate websites, they will attract more of those audiences seeking them, and you'll be less likely to bore or scare away the fans and prospective book buyers for your other genre books.

Blogs and Blogging

Yep, you need to blog. It's part of your platform. Be careful who you are blogging to though. If your blogs talk about writing to other writers, you're really wasting your time. Having other writers to commiserate and connect with for support and camaraderie is nice, but it doesn't build book sales. If I bought every book written by every author I know, I'd have several thousand books. The facts are the facts. Authors do not represent a large portion of your book sales. They never will. Be sure all your blogging efforts are targeted to your fans and prospective book buyers.

Blog no more than every two weeks, and no less than once each month. Choose a day of the week, (Tuesday, Wednesday, or Thursday are best for response) and be consistent. If your blog is posted every other Wednesday and you let everyone know, your following will grow. People will begin to watch for your blog entries and talk about them. Consistency builds everything from bridges to book fans. It's not rocket science or magic. It's common sense.

What to blog? If you really intend to connect with your prospective book buyers and fans, you have to blog about the elements inside your book that will attract them. No one cares about your great aunt's sugar cookie recipe unless you have written a cookbook and your prospective book buyer is a cook book buyer or foodie. Stick to subjects and topics inside your book when you blog.

Social Networking

You need to use Twitter and Facebook. You need to be consistent. You need to belong to groups and organizations. You need to be involved to be visible. But wait, you also need to have time to write, right?

There is a solution. Good social network building strategies and great time management make this all work.

Again, be cautious of how many other authors and writers are among your friends and followers. No, I don't want you to un-friend or block them, but I do want you to reach the correct ratio. For every one author or writer following you on Twitter or friending you on Facebook, you need ten (yes TEN) fans or prospective book buyers. If you've built your following correctly, you can move on to far more efficient tweeting and Facebooking. Here's an example:

- **Twitter** – You have the right ratio of writers to readers and prospective book buyers so every time you tweet, people interested in responding are seeing your tweets. When you tweet about your newest blog post, more of your followers will read it, comment on it and retweet it. What might have been inefficient and ineffective Twitter time is now far more powerful. Never tweet about anything that has nothing to do with your book. No one cares what you ate for lunch or that you just cleaned the toilet. Be social, but not overly social. Interact but make it count.
    - o **Twitter Time Management** – It's so simple you won't believe it. Get on at 10:00 in the morning and again at 2:00 in the afternoon. Spend ten to fifteen minutes each time, tweet away, be efficient and effective, make a few new followers, then simply log off. If you are only on Twitter twenty to thirty minutes a day, Monday through Friday, and you have a listening, eager following, things will happen. Also, you won't tend to get caught up in the social aspect of the twitterverse. Get on, do your thing, and get off. I actually use a kitchen timer to remind myself to log off.
- **Facebook** – This one is also very simple. Correct your ratio of writers and authors to fans and prospective book buyers, then simply use your Facebook page as a way of telling those friends what you want them to know. It's the place to announce your newest blog entry, the place to upload your newest book cover, to tell people where you've been reviewed or where you're appearing. Facebook, when talking to the right crowd of friends, is an extremely powerful marketing tool. Like Twitter and blogging, you must be consistent with Facebook. Every morning, Monday through Friday, post a Facebook question of the day, or fact of the day, or interest of the day. Make sure those posts have something to do with your book's subject or characters. For example, if your write Victorian historic romance, your post of the day could be   a

different picture of clothing or shoes from the Sears and Roebucks catalog from that time period. If you write nonfiction about traveling the world, you can do a daily post of the weather somewhere in the world. Be creative and connect with your fans and prospective book buyers.

- o **Facebook Time Management** – Post your post for the day and maybe one other post if you've blogged or have news, and just pop in occasionally to respond to comments. That's it. You shouldn't spend more than fifteen minutes a day, Monday through Friday, on Facebook.

So now you're wondering about the weekends, right? I never do any social networking on the weekends. I find it too full of crazy people let loose from their cramped offices and more interested in the latest Twitter and Facebook trends than what I have to say. I spend the weekends plotting out my blogs in series and prewriting a few to stay ahead of the load. You might find the weekends productive for your social networking or book subject and I encourage you to test your efforts. Try announcing on Twitter that you are giving away a free copy of your book to the tenth person to post or friend you on your Facebook page. If it works, you should actively social network on the weekends. It might be a perfect technique for your genre and audience.

MARKETING

Let's keep this very simple because marketing is very simple. Marketing is creating awareness for you and your book. Period. Awareness, not sales activity, not promotion, not merchandising, just awareness. How you market can be simple or it can be very intricate and complex. It all depends on how far you are willing to go to create awareness for your book.

When do you market? The moment you decide to write that book is great, but after the book is released is also vital. Everything in between is important too. Your marketing could be a blog that explores your experience of researching your book's subject or location or various story elements. Your marketing can be creating a Twitter circle of followers who love the genre and subject you're writing about. Your marketing can be building Facebook friends who get excited about your coming book. These things are all the action of simple marketing and creating awareness, but there are a few other cogs in the marketing machine that you need to know and respect.

- **Consistency** – Be consistent with your following and friend building by making sure you're collecting followers and friends interested in buying your book (not just other authors). Be consistent with your message, don't vacillate and say one thing about your book being a mystery, then two days later tell everyone it's a romance. Know your message. Be consistent with your timing. Blog religiously at least every other week and on the same day of the week each time. Twitter every day for at least ten minutes twice each day. Your followers will know when you're there and when they can chat with you. Facebook every single day and keep it simple. Avoid the social media traps, just because it's called social media does not mean it social play time. Limit and control your time. Ask a question of the day or create a message of the day on your Facebook and be sure to end your posts with an open-ended question to invite comments. Do this for your blog posts too. Spend no more than ten minutes each day on Facebook, just briefly pop in to respond to comments every few hours. Marketing with consistency means you are reliable and followers want that.

- **Honesty** – Tell the truth. Will it be a mystery or a romance? Are you planning a series? Anything and everything you say in your marketing should be honest. Understandably, some mysteries do morph into a romance during the plotting and writing process, but that change will be part of your journey and the followers and friends you collect will stand by you through it all, as long as it's the truth. Never tell someone you are planning a series when you know it'll be a stand alone. Never announce that you want to create a fundraising event for a charity then drop the ball. Honesty and consistency go hand in hand. The last thing you want to do is lose your followers because they can't trust what you say.

- **Productivity** – If you tell people you are writing a book, you better be writing a book. Writing a book can be a long tedious process, finding literary agent representation or a publishing contract can take a while. Choosing to self-publish requires a learning curve for formatting, or time for locating excellent editors and formatters. Your followers understand that this won't happen overnight, but they are willing to stand by you and be excited for you as long as you don't suddenly change your mind and decided to become a baker halfway through researching your plot. Followers want to see production and hear news. Does your critique group love your concept? Share it. Did your pitch go well at a writers conference? Tell your followers. Are you sending out queries and getting rejections? Share that too. Did you discover new things about your story's location or history that will be part of your book? Tell your followers. They will cheer for you and encourage you and best of all, if you are consistent, honest and being productive, they will be standing in line, waiting to buy your book when it comes out.

Without following these three rules, you are not marketing, all you're doing is making noise and we all know there's more than enough noise out there in the world. Marketing is all about getting a message out to the right people and making them aware that you are writing a book that will someday be sold, or have written a book that is already for sale. We've all heard about the famous 1775 ride of Paul Revere. "One if by land and two if by sea" was the message that night. It was the man in the watch tower's job to get the right message out so that Paul Revere could warn everyone that the British were coming. Imagine if that message was wrong? If it didn't come at all? If it came too late or was unclear? Marketing is about creating awareness. Be the man in the watch tower for your work and market with consistency, honesty and productivity.

PUBLICITY

Marketing is creating awareness, and publicity is the use of the media to get your message out to the public. Marketing and publicity have one thing in common, they can both be done at no cost or on a shoestring budget. Where marketing requires that you connect with friends and followers through Twitter, Facebook, and blogging, publicity works quite differently. Instead of writing blogs, Facebook posts, and tweets, you will be writing press releases.

Publicity requires that you understand the media, how to talk to them, what they will respond to, and most importantly, what is news and what isn't news. Publicity is a completely different game than marketing and in most cases, will only be productive AFTER you have marketed effectively. In other words, it is less likely that a newspaper or publication will respond to your press release unless they have heard something about your project or book first. Good marketing and awareness is the backbone for gaining response and recognition from the public and the media.

Like marketing, there are rules to working with and gaining response from the media for your publicity campaigns.

- **Is it news?** Announcing that you have been signed by a literary agent or publisher is news. Finishing the next chapter is not news. Connecting with a charity that will benefit from a portion of your book's sales is news. Telling the media that you're thinking about contacting a charity to benefit from your book's sales is not news. Reporters and media people are very busy and if they find that the majority of press releases they receive from you are not news, they will begin to automatically discount any press releases from you. We don't want that to happen, so be sure your message is news before you hit the send button.

- **Have you reached the right contact?** There are several ways to reach the media. There's the short cut route, where you simply blast out email press releases to the primary email address for the newspaper, or radio or television station. Then there's the right way. The absolute best way to create the perfect media list for your book is to build it yourself. Research every newspaper, local and national, and locate the appropriate department and reporter complete with their title and direct email address. Move on to magazines and publications and do the same. Now do all the radio and television stations. Don't forget university or college media. When you're finished, you should have a wonderful, massive list of targeted media people to send your press releases to. Some contacts will be in the books and entertainment division and some will be in a department that might relate to your book's unique hook like forestry, green living, or child rearing. Maybe even gardening or cooking and foodies. Never discount the interest of the media in your unique story hooks, they talk to massive numbers of people interested in those unique hooks and can really help if they pick up a story.

- **Is your press release correct?** In *Finding Author Success*, I teach all the elements of writing an effective press release and I strongly suggest you review that information, or pick up a book on writing press releases. The media is filled with busy people who have no time or patience for ill written communication, so it's vital to learn how to write this powerful, clean and succinct form of letter. Who, what, where, why and when is all that goes into your press release, nothing more and nothing less. And always remember to have your contact information in that press release at least twice.

Will you always get response from your press releases? There's no real way to tell because so many factors come in to play. Is it a big news day? Is it a quiet news day? Does the press release have newsworthy impact that might serendipitously connect with other news that day? Have you contacted the correct person? Is it just bad timing? Sometimes you will get a full news story, and other times you'll be ignored. Another thing to keep in mind … it takes time.

Most beginners get little response until after they've proven to their contacts that they are professional, efficient, well marketed, and are not going anywhere. Another thing to understand about the media is that no one will tell you that you've been written about. It's not a secret or meant to be malicious; it's simply that the media has already moved on to the next story. Often a news venue will simply run your press release verbatim and until a friend or associate mentions seeing it, you just might not know. News isn't like being interviewed or purchasing an ad, it runs when it fits best in the media venue's time and space allowances. All that being said, getting a news story can lead to getting more news stories, and that can lead to getting a great story one day. The media is powerful. It can make your career, so it's worth it to email out a few well written and well connected press releases.

As your career moves ahead, the media watches and will become more receptive. It's all a matter of gaining trust and marketing well. If they realize you have created awareness through good marketing, they understand that people are also aware and will read the news story.

PROMOTIONS

Promotion is the activity around which you sell your book. Without creating awareness through marketing, promotion too is destined to fail. Like the media, average people are less likely to respond to something they'd never heard about, so always keep marketing awareness at the top of your priorities.

If marketing is creating awareness and promotion is the activity around which you sell your book, how do you sell your book? The list is endless! Advertising. Participating in events, both book events and events related to the unique hooks inside your story. Creating original events. Holding author events where you do a reading, speak, or do a book signing. Promotions can include merchandising like imprinted mugs or T-shirts, key chains, and book markers. Promotions can be a collaborative effort with other genre writers or other elements that relate to your book. For example, if your fiction has a big focus on green living, you might want to purchase a booth at a local home show to sell and sign your book. If your book connects with young adults, you might want to participate in events designed to attract and entertain young adults.

Promotion is having posters and signage, running contests on your website or participating in contests through other entities related to your genre, prospective book buyer preferences, or businesses related to the subjects in your book.

Promotions can be anything and can have all the sparkly things you want related to it, but it also comes with several words of warning.

Promotions can be very expensive, so build your budget and watch it carefully. Test your results after each promotion and determine if it sold enough books to justify running that particular promotion again. Don't get too wrapped up in what every other author is doing for their promotions because inevitably, it all becomes nothing more than a lot of voices shouting for attention. Choose your promotions carefully and READ THIS BOOK to help you uncover the perfect directions to go where you will have far less competition and can gain far more sales.

PART 2
WHAT IS CROSS MARKETING?

"If you want to succeed you should strike out on new paths, rather than travel the worn paths of accepted success."

~ John D. Rockefeller

Cross marketing isn't supernatural, it isn't some surreptitious passworded process where you need to know the clandestine handshake or swallow live goldfish to learn the secrets of success. It isn't something only highly educated and experienced professionals use when you pay them boatloads of money to make you famous.

Cross marketing is simple and you can do it all by yourself. It's a way of finding multiple markets for your book, no matter the genre or basic target reader. It's a way of digging into your manuscript to mine new readers you never realized were there. It's a way to develop an instinct about writing your next book that allows you to build in a few viable markets *other* authors may not have considered. After all, isn't that the ultimate goal? To gain more readers, more followers, more fans?

Your book is your product and as grand as it is to reach the standard reader – mystery, romance, mystery, horror, supernatural, memoir, or how-to lovers – it's even more exciting to see your readership expand and grow into areas you never imagined.

We're talking about creative, financial, and emotional gratification here, and all you need to do to expand your fan base is follow a few strategies. Cross marketing requires connecting the dots that only you can identify. It takes some serious concentration, but the rewards can be massive. With a little focused commitment and a lot of elbow grease, you can command the readership in your genre.

WHO NEEDS CROSS MARKETING?

Who doesn't need cross marketing is a much better question, and I'm hard pressed to find an answer. Moms use cross marketing to get their kids to eat their veggies. Politicians use it to take people's minds off one issue and focus them onto another. Jeans manufacturers use cross marketing to reach as many possible blue jean buyers in as many different demographics as possible. Automobile manufacturers use it to reach and sell to broad, far reaching customer base. Cross marketing is all around you and at least ten times every day, you are cross marketed to. It's in your email inbox, your snail mailbox, every advertisement you see and every commercial you hear. It isn't exactly bait-and-switch, and it isn't exactly a method of distraction. Cross marketing is a hybrid marketing method of redirecting the marketer's focus to attract wider audiences.

Cross marketing is all about seeing roads to sales targets your competition hasn't identified, and better yet, can't even use. Cross marketing is created for each book and built upon the unique elements within each book. Your book is not the same as another author's book, so the new cross markets you approach will not be overcrowded with yipping, yapping competition. Done right, cross marketing is a way to stand apart and above all your competition.

Here's the best part. It's not actually hard at all. It requires tearing your mind away from the standard thinking most authors use for marketing. It means thinking outside of the box, but in this case, so far outside the box, no other author can ever imitate or catch up with you. The uniqueness of this strategy stems from the distinctiveness of each and every book on the planet. The hardest task ahead is to find those unique elements. I call them your unique hooks and they are the key to all your cross marketing success.

The Cross Marketing Strategies

Mastering the simple strategies for cross marketing isn't difficult. Every industry in the world, no matter what they produce, does the same thing. There's no reason why authors shouldn't take advantage of these processes. In this book we'll be outlining:

- Cross marketing, from the obvious to the sublime
- Crossing the line into TURBO creative thinking
- Taking your platforms to even more effective target markets
- Locating your alternative markets
- How to approach cross markets

- How to maintain new markets

Nothing here is scary to too difficult for an author; after all, you developed a fantastic idea, wrote a whole book and managed to find publication. You can do anything. You're already a successful writer, now it's time to become a successful selling author.

FROM THE OBVIOUS TO THE SUBLIME

I call cross marketing the author's magic because it's so mystically simple, but also extremely deceptive. It's deceptive because the important elements of this strategy seem to be hidden, like a magician's illusions. The key is to open your mind and forget everything any other author in the world ever did to market a book.

P.T. Barnum wanted his circus to be the biggest and the best, so he used cross marketing to attract as many different kinds of people into the big top as possible. Rich and poor, old and young, curious and skeptical all flocked to the ticket booth and paid for the show. You can do the same thing to bring many, many different readers to your book.

To help explain this, let's start with a simple unrelated subject.

Imagine you've just inherited a pizza oven and rented the perfect little location on an active neighborhood street. You've decided to make pizzas. Woo hoo! You're going to be rich! Everyone loves pizza, right? Nope. As unbelievable as it sounds, not everyone out there adores red sauce, pepperoni, and melted mozzarella cheese on fresh baked dough. You're barely making ends meet and need to gain more customers or you'll be out of business soon. You have a competitor a few blocks down the street so you go take a look at what they're doing. They're serving the same kind of pizza and they're hopping busy every day. So what's the problem?

The problem is that your competition has been established and has loyal patrons. What's a pizza marketer to do? Cross market.

The first thing you must do is take a look at who loves pizza

- Young adults and college students
- Young working parents who appreciate the convenience
- Pizza aficionados who tour the city for the best pizza

- Foodies who seek the unusual
- Health buffs and vegetarians
- Kids

Now you must uncover why they go to a specific pizza shop

- Is it for the price?
- Is it for the quality?
- Is it for the uniqueness of the service or atmosphere?

You learn that your prices are competitive, your quality is high and you have a comfortable store with great service. Now what?

It's time to look for ways to bring in more customers while making sure to return loyalty to those who come to your shop regularly.

Let's take this one target at a time.

- **Young adults and college students.** Protect the price for this target because they don't have as much discretionary income. Look for things those young adults love in other parts of their life and connect it with your shop and pizza. Perhaps you can have a Teen Hour or College Night where the music is loud and fun. You can hold contests to win a free pizza party or tickets to rock concerts.
- **Young working parents.** Maybe it's a good idea to have a designated employee between the hours of five and six p.m. for taking phone, text, on-line, or fax orders so that the pizzas are ready for pick up or delivered at the perfect time.
- **Pizza aficionados.** Perhaps you can create a competition between all the local pizza shops to raise money for a charity, kind of like American Idol only with pizza. That will get the aficionados' attention.
- **Foodies.** If you've decided this is a lucrative customer, you'll need to add special foodie items to your menu. Toss some fresh basil or rosemary into your pizza dough; top the pizza with unique sauces and ingredients. Maybe add a dessert pizza, something with a whipped cream cheese sauce topped with fresh seasonal fruits and sprinkled with chunky, crystallized sugar.
- **Health buffs and Vegetarians.** This requires healthy menu choices that cater to those customers. Whole wheat pizza dough, great   fresh

veggies, and wonderful seasonal produce can help with this target.

- **Kids.** Like McDonalds, you can do a few super kid-friendly things. Offer catered kid parties, have kid-sized personal pizzas on the menu, design the little pizzas with a pepperoni smiling face.

Next you must make sure all those new targets know about your activities to serve them.

- Walk around and give away discount coupons targeted to each of your new menu features
- Give away free sample bites to everyone who walks past your door
- Take kiddy pizzas to one of the local little league games for the players to enjoy
- Place an ad in the foodie, health buff, and vegetarian publications
- Make sure your signage lists your weekly events and who those events are targeted for so that passers-by can see it and make note

NOW you've taken your pizza shop and reached six new highly targeted customers than you originally had.

As you know, anyone can make a pizza, good, bad, or boring – and in this day and age, anyone can write and publish a book, good, bad, or boring. The competition for the book buyer's dollar is big, so making sure you reach as many audiences as possible is one of the great keys to success. You have strong, long established competition right in your genre. You have difficulties with reaching new book buyers and you have the same challenges the pizza shop has. But, as you can see, it's all about what's on the pizza or in the book that makes the difference.

Okay, now back to cross marketing for authors. (Just give me a minute to lick the sauce from my fingers.)

Genre Games

Let's say you've written a romance. Everyone loves romance, right? After all, it is the biggest selling genre in the world. But just setting up shop and announcing that your romance is being released won't be enough. Of course you will reach the avid romance readers looking for new authors but will that be enough either?

Start with your subgenre. Is it paranormal romance? Is it YA romance? Contemporary? Science fiction or futuristic or even historical romance? Is it erotic romance? Does it have a mystery element in the story, making it a hot mystery romance? Playing the genre game is very important when planning your cross marketing strategies.

There are ways to stretch the limits of a genre. Granted, for sales purposes, on websites and in bookstores as well as seeking a literary agent, you must be very clear on the genre. The trick to cross marketing well is to always think about what happens beyond those limited categories, and who out there might love your book.

If your book is an urban fantasy with romance in it, why can't you market to romance readers? If your book is about romance with a werewolf, there's no reason you can't cross market that paranormal romance with general romance. We're talking about subtle approaches here, not slam-bam crashing into the door of a traditional romance reader's book club or a reviewer and insisting they'll love your book. There's a careful strategy to approaching cross market targets and that's not it. Research carefully. If a book club or reading group or even a book reviewer specifically says they want romance, dig deeper. You'll discover that romance is romance and falls under several subgenres. The key here is to reach readers your primary genre *isn't* reaching. Much more on this later when we will delve into something I call SUPER Genres, to help make genre gaming even more powerful for you.

The Meat

So, where's the meat? For this strategy, it really *doesn't* matter what your genre or subgenre is. This cross marketing strategy is completely determined by WHAT'S INSIDE YOUR BOOK. You wrote this book and even though you may not have known it at the time, you've already written your cross markets into it. Just take a long, deep look at your manuscript. Where are the cross markets?

Does your main character love to cook? If so, no matter what kind of book you've written (romance, mystery, urban fantasy), cooking supply stores, cooking clubs, cooking schools, cooking tools websites, and blogs about cooking could represent great cross markets for you.

Does your main character live in a specific historic or destination part of the world? Now you can cross market to the museums, welcome centers, gift shops, and travel websites for that location.

Does your main character travel, eat donuts, love chocolate, or live on the beach or in the mountains?

Have I made my point? The sublime magic of cross marketing is to go places other authors don't bother to go to reach readers. If your character loves coffee, there's no reason you can't ask coffee shops to permit you to have a book signing, or post a daily comment on their website to promote your book. Each day you can mention the daily brew and if your homicide detective main character likes it, or which pie he prefers, or even what newspaper he's reading while enjoying his coffee.

Good cross marketing is about seeing beyond the average and digging deep into your manuscript to find those possible magical markets. They're yours for the plucking simply because there is no competition with other books or authors, AND there's no competition with the product you're connecting with. As long as the coffee store continues to gain customers, they're happy. And if you gain book buyers, everybody is happy!

Around the Pizza in Eighty Days!

So you thought pizza and cross marketing were not connected? Check out this global pizza cross marketing …

Around the world, pizza toppings vary greatly, reflecting regional tastes and preferences. In Japan, for instance, eel and squid are favorites. In Pakistan, curry is a big seller. In Russia, red herring is the topping of choice. Australians enjoy shrimp and pineapple as well as barbeque toppings on their pizza pies. Costa Ricans favor coconut.

~ Source: Numero Uno Pizzeria

Some of the more popular international toppings are pickled ginger, minced mutton and tofu in India; squid and Mayo Jaga (mayonnaise, potato and bacon) in Japan; and green peas in Brazil. In Russia, they serve pizza covered with mockba; a combination of sardines, tuna, mackerel, salmon and onions. In France, a popular combo is called the Flambee with bacon, onion, and fresh cream.

~ Source: Domino's Pizza

TURBO CREATIVITY THINKING 101

How creatively do you really think?

As writers, we are free thinkers and do our best not to focus on the rules while we create, but those rules are there, looming even bigger if we're just getting started as an author. If you're attempting to gain a literary agent, there are all the query rules, format rules, and acceptable approaches rules to consider. There are the rules about clean genre, clean manuscripts, and clean elevator pitches. If we're going the independent or small publisher route, they have their own set of requirements and each one is different. If you self-publish, there are perfect editing necessities, a formatting learning curve and of course, all the distribution and promotional systems to master.

With all these rules floating around, crowding and confusing the process from the finished, beautifully imaginative novel you wrote to the actual book sales, how creative can one really be? It's as though the course of action we must take simply chokes the creativity out of us. There are so many tiny commandments to follow; it's too easy to get sidetracked into pleasing the process and forgetting the book buyer.

I'm here to talk about breaking those patterns we learned in nursery school where marketing is concerned. *Don't* follow the rules. *Don't* worry about being correct. *Don't* question the process I'm about to suggest, because if you do, you may just find yourself spending more time satisfying the system and never reaching your own goals.

Before we begin, I will apologize. I am from the sixties. It's time for a little REVOLUTION in the author marketing process. It's time to tap into all the beautiful colors and emotions and excitement you felt while writing your book. Frankly, if you don't recapture and convey that intensity, why should anyone want to read your book, much less pay for it?

See, it's not always just the perfect crafting of a 10 word sound bite or 25 word elevator pitch that gets someone's interest, it's the author's energy. That flash of excitement can and should be in those few words, but it also must be present in the process the author uses to communicate with the prospective buyer.

It's time for a little mind-blowing magical mystery tour. Yes, this will seem weird for anyone born after 1975 but it will be fun. AND, it's vital! I'm going to ask you to take ten minutes out of your crazy day to just sit and clear your thoughts. Come on, you can spare a few minutes away from Twitter, Facebook, your iPhone, and texting. This is important and it's most important you do it AWAY from your technology. Go outside and sit in the grass if you can. I know it sounds silly but really, when your book idea came to you, what did you do? Get onto Twitter and Facebook? Text the world that you have an idea? My bet is that you didn't even sit at your keyboard right away. You sat someplace quiet and you thought. I need you to get back to that emotional space. Be peaceful. Clear everything else from your mind. Breathe nice and even, meditate for a few moments if you can. Now that you're there, you can start.

Recall the process of developing your story and how it came to you, all the curves and u-turns it took before it became the final novel. Feel the characters, what you like and don't like about each one, explore the emotions then plant yourself firmly into the locations. Even if your book is fantasy, science fiction, or deep historic, get yourself there, feel it, smell it, taste it. No grumbling. If you went this route to develop your story, it's not new to you. If you love your story, it's no hardship. Most importantly, if you reconnect this way, everything about marketing and cross marketing the astounding book you wrote will be that much closer to you. So get into this. I promise it will be rewarding.

Now come back from your journey slowly so that you can retain the magic. Examine what you brought back with you. While still sitting quietly, jot down the biggest impressions you received. Now set it aside and do the whole thing again for ten minutes the next day, and the next. Do this for four or five days then collect your jotted notes and begin.

If your goal is to seriously attack and gain visibility and sales for your book, this process may seem a little bohemian, but just go with me.

Start with the biggest impression. Perhaps it was *Green*. Maybe your book is about ecology, or raising milk cows, or a romance about a playground planner falling for a beautiful politician who hates kids, but *Green* was the impression you wrote down. The key here is *Green*. If *Green* stuck with you, it will stick with readers. The goal is to get more readers than the average marketing strategy will reach. Let's play a mind stretching game and find a few cross markets you might have never thought of. How many people can you capture with *Green*? Let your mind flow from the key word out as far as it will go.

- **Green** – plants, the color, ecological organizations, paint stores, interior decorators
- **Park** – city parks, town parks, park developers, art parks, car parks, antique car clubs
- **Farm** – dairy farm, farm markets, vineyards, wine gift stores, wine tasting gatherings
- **Garden** – gardening clubs, on-line gardening groups, florists, flower arranging schools
- **Herbs** – cooking, chefs, culinary schools, cooking gadget stores, cookbook clubs
- **Forest** – forestry groups, camping groups, Robin Hood, survival groups

- **Mountain** – camping, hiking, rafting, skiing, climbing, wildlife preservation
- **Money** – teaching, becoming the expert, cross marketing, making BIG sales

That last one is me, getting you back to practicality, but first let's talk about the other ideas. As you can see, some of these directions went way off track, but did they? Can they possibly work for your book? The idea here is not to think logically, but to let a concept like *Green* flow into as many different directions as you can find. Play with this. Laugh at it. Enjoy this process because that's a big part of regaining your joy for the book you wrote.

Getting back to feeling the creative process of writing your book is the only, I repeat, the *ONLY* road to being creative with cross marketing your book. Using strategies and tried-and-true systems are good, but combining them with TURBO creative direction is the key to success.

Now, of the ideas above, if the book is a romance about a playground planner falling for a beautiful politician who hates kids, let's see how many of the impressions and ideas above could work. Aside from the standard romance avenues for marketing, you can now cross market to:

- Playground designers, planners, and associations
- Safe and ecological playground and park organizations
- Teachers and daycares
- Parents
- City, county, and local community center bookstores
- Vineyards and wine gift stores (for the romance aspect)
- Gardening clubs
- Romantic cookbook stores or cooking classes

You can speak about safe playgrounds or ecology, or cooking for children, or making romance part of everyday life, or including kids in helping in the garden or in the kitchen – in other words, you can become the expert on these subjects and speak to parents, single parents or community clubs.

Not one of these ideas falls into the standard romance marketing category because NOW you're thinking about cross marketing and thinking about it in a productive way.

All right, you can put away your bellbottoms, tie-died T-shirt, and headband now.

NICHE MARKETS

There are two paths to creating truly effective alternate marketing strategies and both are important. Cross marketing and niche marketing.

Niche marketing is all about finding unique, usually small but powerful target markets for your book. There are niche markets somewhere inside your manuscript whether its fiction or nonfiction. This is how big selling authors keep gaining more sales. Not by repeatedly pounding at the same audience, but by locating new audiences in different places.

Throughout this book niche marketing and cross marketing will apply and be the basis for your strategies, so it's important to understand what a niche market actually is. A niche market can be:

- Dog lovers, cat lovers, or animal lovers
- Economics
- Politics
- Bakers or cooks
- Psychics
- The Medical, military, or legal industry
- Parenting for families, foster families, young families, or single parents
- Religion, faith, or spirituality
- Health and fitness
- Or a million other things

You locate these niche markets in your manuscript by seeking out the tone of the book, whether it's the personal focus or quirk of a character or plot. It could even be a secondary focus for a nonfiction book.

For example, if your fiction has a main character who loves his dog or works with dogs as a secondary plot element, dog lovers may be your perfect niche market. Finding your niche market has nothing to do with your genre or subgenre, but has everything to do with unique hooks and focuses of character or story.

If your nonfiction is about a clutter free organization, your niche markets might be home owners, parents, teachers, or small business owners.

Keep in mind, your niche market isn't the main focus of your book … it's the flavor or music under the main story or nonfiction subject that has enough effect on the book to clearly make it interesting to people in that niche market.

CROSS MARKETS

Cross marketing is a strategy designed to find more of your existing target markets in different ways and places than standard marketing.

Cross markets are slightly different than niche markets. Cross marketing will seek a larger reader base in different places than your competition (who are all shouting to book clubs and genre reader groups). Here are a few examples of what cross markets might be:

- Romance – Women found in woman's auxiliary groups, nursing groups, gardening clubs, or exercise classes
- Science fiction – People found in teaching groups, technology, science clubs, or organizations
- Urban fantasy, paranormal, supernatural or fantasy books – Based on the target demographic of course (i.e. men, women, young adults) you will look for places where lovers of these specific genres spend time. For example, at vampire discussion boards, in supernatural or paranormal groups, and don't forget the general places people go to be together – cooking clubs, bicycling clubs, skiing clubs, etc.
- Nonfiction – If your book is about nutrition, spread your approaches toward the health conscious at health clubs, parents, even cooking clubs and foodies, as well as nursing groups and teachers groups. If your nonfiction subject is ecological in nature, think about all the groups of people who, although the reason they gather may not be related, still care about ecology.

Older than You Think!

The first record that man used magic for creating success dates back to over fifty-two thousand years ago. Magic was practiced by cavemen as evidenced by many of the cave drawings. By drawing the scenes of conquest over an animal, it gave them power through self-confidence, which was thus believed to be magic and create victory in the hunt.

WIZARDRY ASSIGNMENT

Take a moment to think about your own book. You might even want to take   a weekend and reread it, just to refresh your memory about everything that's inside the story. Can you identify your niche markets and your cross markets? Remember, a niche market is a unique, usually small but strong target market found inside your story. A cross market is locating MORE of your existing target market in different ways and places than standard marketing will reach. Make lists under each category and set them aside until you've moved on and read a few more sections of this book. Once you have an understanding about how to approach these niche and cross markets, review the list and determine if these ideas are still viable. Can they be better? Stronger? More Creative?

PART 3
EXPANDING YOUR PLATFORMS

"Apparently wizards poke their noses in everywhere!"
~ J.K. Rowling, Harry Potter and the Deathly Hallows

In order to help you understand how to tap into these new niche markets and cross markets, we're going to begin with helping you understand the ways you can expand your platforms.

I know, I hear you. Your immediate reaction to this is something like … "OMG, I already have websites and blogs and guest blogging responsibilities *and* Facebook and Twitter to deal with! Please don't tell me I have to create MORE venues for my platforms!"

No. No new venues to create. This works much more simply than that. Have you ever heard the phrase, "making money with other people's money"? Well this is kind of like that. No, you won't be stealing friends and fans or ideas from other authors' platforms, but this strategy helps you gain fans and book buyers from other group, business and association platforms.

Just a reminder before we begin, **niche marketing** is all about finding a unique, usually small but strong target market for your book. **Cross marketing** is a strategy designed to find more of your existing target markets in different ways and places than standard marketing.

Okay, let's start.

NONFICTION NICHE AND CROSS MARKETS

Let's take a nonfiction book about how to be organized. Let's imagine the book primarily talks about organizing drawers or closets and storage space. The primary target market for this book is homeowners who want to be organized.

Imagine that the niche markets include:

- #1 niche market – kitchens (women)
- #2 niche market – garages (men)
- #3 niche market – home offices and businesses (entrepreneurs)

And imagine that the cross markets include:

- #1 cross market – schools, teachers
- #2 cross market – daycares, doggie daycares
- #3 cross market – crafting, sewing, gardening and arts groups
- #4 cross market – where ever people gather, meetings, clubs and organizations
- #5 cross market – volunteer and church groups

Now, what you see here is that a nonfiction book primarily written to help people organize their lives at home, has grown a large extended market for promotion and exposure. Even though the primary target reader for this book is homeowners, niche marketing will expose the book to new readers in smaller but strong target markets. It reaches out to women who want organized kitchens and men who love their garage sparkling neat and organized. It also reaches out to small businesses, all in an effort to touch niche markets that can benefit from the strategies in the book. It seeks out an additional direction with entrepreneurial groups, knowing that the organizational skills taught in the book can help new business people.

The cross markets listed for this book simply seeks out more prospective book buyers for the book in different environments. It takes into consideration that even though people like to be organized at home, they might like to be more organized at work if they are teachers or daycare workers, at play if they craft or garden or paint, and wherever they meet for a purpose. The goal with cross marketing is to reach these people where they are and show them why they want this book.

FICTION NICHE AND CROSS MARKETS

Let's say your book is a contemporary woman's fiction, covering   the emotional journey of your main character from difficult times to a good life. Let's take this further and say that the story has several unique hooks. It takes place in small Vermont town, that the main character raises horses and loves everything about the pristine nature of the state of Vermont which has no billboards, is very green (physically and ecologically), and boasts small town charm. Let's imagine that the primary plot point for this particular book is the main character's recovery from a terrible accident that leaves her in a wheelchair. Your primary target market for this book is women.

Imagine that the niche markets include:

- #1 niche market – horses
- #2 niche market – physical rehabilitation
- #3 niche market – small town life
-

And cross markets include:

- #1 cross market – anywhere women gather or meet
- #2 cross market – travel agencies
- #3 cross market – green or ecology groups
- #4 cross market – horse lovers groups
- #5 cross market – women working in offices, hospitals or other businesses
-

Now that you've identified your niche and cross market targets, where are these people? To approach this task, I'm going to give you a possible solution for a niche market and cross market for both the nonfiction organization book, and the women's fiction. But remember, it's vital that you identify where you can reach these markets live and on-line in order to begin the process of approaching and maintaining them.

Nonfiction about Organization
Niche Market – Kitchens

Okay, since this is a niche market and targets people who love an organized kitchen, here are a few ways to approach this market.

- You can contact kitchen designer websites and offer to write a monthly article about kitchen organization for them, provided they permit you to show a book cover and have the buy link for the book at the bottom of your monthly article. Keep in mind that these will not be articles   about the author's book. They will be articles about organizing a kitchen by the author of that book. NOTE: If two or more different businesses like the idea of you doing this kind of thing, YOU CANNOT REPEAT CONTENT. You will need to be creative with your offerings to the business. For example, one will have a monthly article about organizing kitchens, a second may have a Q&A, (like an Ask the Organizing Expert), and the third might feature pictures of before and after the organization skills taught in the book are applied.

- You may want to talk to local consumer cooking schools, the kind that teach regular people how to cook. Most cities have some variations on these schools. You can propose speaking engagements as a kitchen organizing class, you can offer to sell your book at a discount to their students, hold book signings after a class, or perhaps you can do the same kind of articles you're doing with the kitchen designer websites at the schools website or blog.

Cross Market – Daycares

- For this cross marketing target, you'll need to find the places daycare workers gather. Seek out blogs that focus on daycare, Yahoo! Groups that discuss daycare, and meetings about daycare in your community. Locate daycare chains and church daycares. Once you've found these groups, choose what you'll do to get them to consider your book. You can speak at meetings about organization and how the book helps people in the daycare industry. You can offer daycare and child rearing bloggers a blog series about the subject (with your book cover and buy link at the bottom). You can join Yahoo! Groups and offer tidbits of organizational wisdom to the group – and of course your book cover and buy link will always appear at the bottom of your email.

Genre, Women's Fiction
Niche Market – Small Town Life

Now this particular niche market expands the general market from Vermont to a much larger target of small town life. This doesn't mean that big city people aren't interested in small town life, it simply means that you've chosen this as a niche market.

- You can contact targeted on-line and hard print magazines and publications about writing an article or monthly column about small town life. Your bio will appear at the bottom of these articles or columns as well as your buy links for the book. Again, these are not articles about your book. They are articles about the subject of small town life and speaking to an audience interested in small town life. Remember, YOU CANNOT REPEAT CONTENT. Be creative and make sure that the ideas you offer each venue for your articles or columns are different from the other magazines or publications.

- Reach out to bloggers who focus on small town lifestyle and offer to guest blog or offer them a series as a guest blogger. Again, always use original content.

Cross Market – Green or Ecological Groups

- Cross marketing is all about adding readers to your fan base. Seek out Yahoo! Groups, chat boards, and live groups in your area who focus on ecological subjects. Offer to speak live, share your thoughts on a green lifestyle and talk about how your commitment to ecological matters plays out in your book. Look for on-line businesses that sell green products and offer to do a green tip every month if they'll let you add your book cover and buy link to the bottom. Take flyers about your book to farmer's markets or state fairs where living green is a way of existence. Imagine this target until they're clear in your head, then go wherever they might be.

As you can see, the ways to approach a niche market and a cross market are the same strategies, but the key to all marketing is to identify your targets in order to reach out to them.

LOCATING YOUR ALTERNATIVE MARKETS

Where do you find readers for your book? How to you search for them and how can you know which avenue will be successful and which will be a bust?

Imagine you're in an unfamiliar city and need to make a purchase at the grocery store. As similar and organized as grocery stores across the country can be, you simply can't find the product you're looking for. Say you want a pound of coffee. Usually it's on the shelves with tea and dry coffee creamers, but in this store, you just can't locate it. Where would you look? With the baking goods? The cake mixes and sugar? Perhaps it's in the aisle with the cookies and packaged cakes? Maybe it's with the cereals and dry breakfast items. Could it be with the breads? Maybe this particular store has a special aisle just for hot   coffee beverages, specialty imported coffees, hot chocolate mixes and flavored coffees? If you still can't find it, you might try the bakery section of the store because they may have set up a coffee display along the beautiful fresh baked goods.

In other words, where might you find the coffee? If you think hard enough, you can probably determine ten or fifteen fairly logical places for the store to stock their coffee cans.

It's the same with your book. Just because it's a pound of coffee doesn't mean there's only one place to display it. If you dissect your manuscript, you will find several different possible places to find your prospective book buyer, readers, and fans.

To find alternative markets for your book, you must revisit everything in your book. Make a list of every possible alternative reader you can think of then do even deeper exploration.

For example, let's try this with a random book.

- **Genre** – Murder mystery/historic
- **Location** – Eastern seaside town, 1910
- **Plot Point 1** – The murder takes place in a lighthouse
- **Plot Point 2** – The town suspects an elderly man of the murder
- **Character 1 Preferences** – Detective chews black licorice and smokes cigars
- **Character 2 Preferences** – His wife, the protagonist who has an instinct that the elderly man is innocent, is a gardener who discovers the murder weapon in her own petunia patch
- **Standard Interest Groups** – Mystery lovers and mystery book clubs. Historic book lovers and historic book clubs.
- **Cross Marketing Target Groups** – Lighthouse lovers, tourist websites to lighthouses and seaside locations. Cigar websites. Licorice and candy websites. Gardening groups and gardening supply websites.
- **On-line Exposure Possibilities** – Create a simple blog just for the book and connect with all the groups listed above through your social networking. Build a careful following on Facebook and Twitter with these kinds of groups, and every time you blog in that special blog, let all your friends and followers know. Contact the websites listed above - lighthouse lover blogs and websites, tourist websites, cigar websites, licorice and candy websites, and gardening supply websites - and either become active in their discussions or ask to do a monthly offering and post your book on their websites. Do the same with lighthouse, cigar, candy, and gardening websites and bloggers. On your book platform

website, develop a page specifically to attract lighthouse lovers. Create a blog just for lighthouse lovers, cigar lovers, or garden lovers and build new fans there by promoting your book after each entry.

- **Publicity Angle** – Historic lighthouses need funding support for maintenance
- **Media** – After deciding to create a fundraiser or participate in a fundraiser to support historic lighthouses, sent out standard press releases to all eastern seaside town papers and magazines

All right, this is a great list, but is it reasonable? Perhaps your detective character really does love cigars, but you know nothing about cigars. Perhaps cigars, attracting mostly a male buyer, would be the wrong audience to go after for your book which is written to attract mostly female readers. What if the licorice direction can prove very lucrative? Maybe you located a specialty licorice company with a really cool website and they're thrilled to have your book featured there. Look what you've got! You get to sell books to new readers and there's no competition between you and the candy maker.

Now, take a serious look at the lighthouse element. The power of this particular approach is that all along the eastern and western seaboard and the Great Lakes there are lighthouses. These structures have been a fascination for over a century to many, many people. There are huge organizations of lighthouse lovers who dedicate their time and money to visiting, climbing, and supporting the maintenance of lighthouses. This is an extremely good direction to go. Getting involved with a fundraiser for these organizations on a local or even national level can only help expose your book in a big way to a big new readership.

On-line, you'll need to really play with your cross markets. Don't just join a Yahoo! Group for lighthouse lovers and announce that you've written a book, get involved with the group. Chat. Make friends. Always have your email tag with your book title and buy link visible and let it do the selling for you. In groups like that, people buy from friends, not interlopers who pop in, talk about themselves and their products then leave.

Make sure your author and book websites are active with lots of interesting information so that possible book buyers come back regularly to see what's new. Regarding a blog, yes, you want a book blog, but be sure to create a blog category about lighthouses because this can do something magical for you. It can establish you as an expert of sorts.

The goal is to help you locate and connect with your possible cross markets. Dig deep into your manuscript and make your own list like the one above. Let yourself go wild with it, you never know where there might be a fantastic hidden alternative market you never thought about before. After you've developed the list, bring a critical eye to it. What will not work? What markets are simply too time consuming and difficult to approach? What seems like a simple market to approach? What feels right and what feels wrong? You know your book intimately and only you can dissect it and find the cross marketing gems inside. Make your list and sleep on it.

PITCHING NICHE AND CROSS MARKETS

Ah, the pitch. We all know it well, we do it all the time as authors, and reaching out to niche and cross markets is no different. A standard pitch is nice, but with anything, carefully designing your pitch for the person receiving it is most effective. When we pitch a literary agent or publisher, we're trying to impress them with our writing ability, our book concept, and our background. When seeking reviews, our pitch is a little different. Those pitches focus solely on the book, its genre, target reader, powerful plot, and interesting characters. We need to make the reviewer want to read our book. When we write a press release about our book, the goal is to interest the media on how our book impacts the world through our publicity and public relations activities. We're giving them news. So, how does one pitch a niche or cross market?

There are three important elements to pitching niche and cross markets effectively, but only one goal. That goal is to create a win/win situation. Without that, you will fail. So before approaching a niche or cross market, be sure to cover the following three points.

Have a plan
- Determine your target niche or cross market. Let's imagine you've determined that your niche market is chocolate, and your cross market is chocolate lovers. You know you want to reach out to chocolate lovers because the main character in your humorous romance entitled *For Love or Chocolate* is a hopeless chocoholic. You've determined that this unique element within your manuscript is strong enough, and reaches your primary demographic, men. Now you need a plan.
- Research. Begin with research and start that research in your own back yard. Is there a candy maker or candy store in your neighborhood, town, or city? Take a little road trip and look around. Are the   majority

of their displayed products made with chocolate? Or is it primarily other things like jelly beans or licorice? Is there enough chocolate in their display cases to justify putting them into your plan? Take that research further and look into the small chain stores. Will they work? Now consider on-line chocolate companies, the kind that deliver lovely boxes of chocolates right to someone's door. Many of these businesses don't have a retail store, so you simply do your research on their websites. Do they qualify? Next you will research the big companies that fit your story. Godiva Chocolate? Yes. Hershey's Chocolate? Maybe not. It all depends on your story.

- Will your offering be original? The next part of your planning has everything to do with exploring these companies to see if anyone else is doing what you hope to do. You want to write a monthly article, or create an interesting chocolate fact of the month on their business websites or newsletters, but you should make sure someone hasn't beaten you to that idea.

- Create six offering ideas. The final part of your plan is to develop six or seven different offerings for your pitch. One might be a monthly column about the tongue-in-cheek health benefits of chocolate. Another might be a monthly article series about the powers of chocolate for the libido. Another idea might be to create a series of articles about the history of chocolate. Maybe one idea is about chocolatiers, chocolate art displays, and competitions. Come up with six ideas you can produce; then move ahead to build your pitches.

Be Precise

- Who are you pitching? As mentioned earlier, all pitches are different depending on who you are pitching to and the reason you're pitching. Just as you would tweak your query for each different literary agent or publisher, you will also make those adjustments for each different business. Being precise is the key to success when pitching niche and cross markets. The first thing you must be precise with is your contact information. Just as you wouldn't randomly choose a publisher to pitch or a random reporter to send a press release to, you wouldn't blindly send off a pitch for your niche or cross marketing efforts. Dig to find the correct contact. In some cases, it might be the owner of the store, in other's the webmaster, in yet others, it might be the company marketing director. You may need to send a few emails to locate the right   person or it may require a personal visit or phone call. Identify who you need to send your pitch to and make careful note of it.

- Does your idea fit? You have a cool idea about the history of chocolate, but you want to pitch it to a new candy company that makes chocolate desserts in a futuristic style. Does this idea fit with this target? You might have more luck offering a fun article series on how chocolate will save the world or fuel space ships, or cure future infestations of jellybean aliens. Design your ideas around the feel and atmosphere of the company you want to pitch. It will not only make them feel special, it will make them feel comfortable with you. If you want to offer a special column series about unique chocolate artisans, you would not want to pitch it to the Mars Candy Company. And if you want to capitalize on the fact that your character loves chocolate candy, you may want to avoid bakeries that feature cupcakes or cookies. Make sure your idea makes sense to the receiver of your pitch.

- Don't ask for too much. Believe it or not, I have seen authors make these approaches to niche and cross markets but immediately sabotage themselves by demanding too much in return. The most you should request is permission to display your book cover and its buy link at the end of your articles. If the articles are intriguing enough and the company wants you to do them, they may offer more, but never ask for more. Demanding a free ad and endorsement as well as an endless contract to tap into their customer base is way out of the question. Yes, the value of what you bring to that candy company might justify it, but be realistic. They aren't interested in selling books, just chocolate. The ONLY way these strategies work is if both the company and the author benefit. Be fair, be realistic, and be friendly. This could grow into a huge boon for you and your chocoholic's romance series or it can melt away quickly. You must always have a good attitude and be ready to shake hands and move on to a different target.

Make it enticing

- Focus on the company. When you've gathered all your information, know the correct contact and exactly what you want to pitch to each company, it's time to prepare your pitch. There are careful approaches to writing this query. First and foremost, focus on the company. If you are proposing a blog series for a candy company's blog, make sure you tell them how much you love their website and embedded blog. Tell them you love their products, and tell them why you feel you can bring value to their on-line presence. This is where you give them your 25 word pitch and explain why you feel your book and their company is a perfect match. After that, you will propose the series topic you would like to offer and what you would like in return. If your hope is to create a series of speaking engagements where you hold events in the candy company's various stores, do live readings then speak on your series topic, explain it all, most especially how you believe that your activities will bring in new customers to them. You might even suggest that the chocolate store allow you to place candy discount coupons inside the books you sign and sell as book marks, thus pulling the book buyer back into the store for another purchase. Everything you put into this pitch must bode favorably for the company because basically, they're doing just fine without you. If you can't bring something beneficial to the table, they will not be interested.

- Make it a win/win. Even if it takes some compromise, make every effort to create a win/win situation. I have seen authors become great friends with a business after cross marketing with them. Wonderful symbiotic relationships can happen, but just as easily the win/win might not be to your advantage. If you find little sales to show for your efforts, you need to move on to a different target. Always watch out for yourself and protect your time. Don't let the company ask for too much and never continue with ineffective efforts.

- Be consistent. If you tell a business that you will do something, do it. I totally understand that an author's life can be complex and busy. We have family responsibilities, dirty dishes, deadlines, and our own muses to deal with, but if you've made a commitment to cross marketing, like a monthly article to a business website, be sure to do it. Nothing destroys mutual faith more than dropping the ball. Be consistent.

HOW FAR IS TOO FAR?

Understanding the effectiveness of niche or cross markets might take a little time. They might build slowly, or explode into massive sales quickly. They might take more of your time than you originally planned for, or they might be easy as pie to keep up with. The company might start out thrilled and excited but slowly lose interest in what you're doing. Or, it might start slow and eventually that company will do anything to keep you happy and involved. The possibilities are endless, but the results are all that matter to you. Are you doing too little? Are you doing too much? And the question is always going to be, how far is too far?

- **Your book is the underline, and not the statement.** Cross marketing is not marketing the way most authors understand marketing. It isn't fireworks and loud speakers and it isn't a quick solution to a problem. Authors have perfected cross marketing by putting hard sell tactics on the back burner. Cross marketing is about making new friends, developing a new market for your book, and being very subtle about it. All of your content for articles or a monthly column must attract and hold the attention of the company's customers, those same customers you want to buy your book. If you entertain them where they are – on a website for people interested in scuba diving or buying scuba equipment – you can easily pull them in with a great scuba article about south pacific weather patterns, then hook them into wanting your mystery about a scuba diver with the picture of your book cover and buy link at the bottom of the story. Never focus your articles or column on your book, always on the company's customers. Plan well, connect with the right venues, and never use hard sell tactics with a cross market.

- **Don't avoid standard marketing, promotions, and publicity.** Yes, this is a book about advanced cross marketing strategies, but that does not give you a free pass on doing all the standard basic marketing strategies, and doing them consistently. You must constantly connect with the audience you already have as well as build new fans into that following. That means a daily effort to build a Twitter following interested in your book's unique hook, and a growing number of Facebook friends who are just discovering your unique story hooks. It means planning and executing several blog series that target prospective book buyers interested in each unique hook. If you've written a book that took place in the sixties, you can have a blog series about music, cloths, and politics of the sixties. All you need to do is close each blog entry with two things – an open-ended question, and your wonderful 25 - 30 word pitch. Pop in your book cover with buy link and voila, you've attracted people interested in sixties bellbottoms or Janice Joplin hits, and they get a look at your book. Always remember, being consistent with your marketing efforts means being faithful to your existing fans and the new ones to come. You can't simply drop the old standard strategies. They must continue in order to support your new cross marketing efforts.

- **Limit the number of venues.** Let's imagine you have five possible cross markets to approach. Your book title is *Stomplin' Boots* and one of those cross markets is country music. You begin by approaching on-line cowboy boot stores, locating the contact, and convincing him to let you write a monthly column entitled *Country Music and Boots*, where you will have a small promotion for your book at the end with a book cover and buy link. He likes it, so you begin. After that you contact a website with a huge fan base for a particular country music star. You contact the owner of the website and propose a monthly article where you write about the song lyrics of the singer and how they fit with everyday life. You tell them you will have a small promotion for your book at the end of each article and they agree. That's a go. Next you find a clothing store that features cowboy chic, and you create an idea for a question of the month for country clothing chic. Questions like "Do these boots go with my wedding gown?" and "The buffalo belt buckle as jewelry". They love the idea and have no issues with you promoting your book. What else should you add? NOTHING. Never try to handle more than three venues at a time. Remember, for each venue you must write and turn in an 800 – 1,000 word article or column on time, you must monitor responses to your article, and you must pay attention to your sales. In addition to all your other blogging, marketing, and promoting, this can become overwhelming, so keep it manageable. Some might only be able to handle two at a time, some might find one enough. Never take on more than you can handle.

- **Market and promote effectively** – It's fantastic that you've gained three wonderful venues that are sure to drive new prospective book buyers to your book! It's wonderful that the managers at the venue are crazy about you and your idea, but always remember, YOU asked for this, not the venue. Don't expect them to market or promote your monthly column. Some may do some marketing because they're committed to the idea and because they're hoping the effort gains more sales and loyalty for them and their products. But generally, it's your job to tell the world what you're doing. You must use Twitter, Facebook, all the on-line groups you belong to, and that mailing list you've been building. If you've built it well, it's loaded with fans and prospective book buyers who will pass your message on to more fans and prospective book buyers. If you belong to groups of country music lovers and country clothing lovers, you may be able to really impress the venues by bringing new customers to them. If you tell the world about your columns, the world will pop over and take a look. Done right, you'll sell more books and the venues will sell more of their products.

- **Have a backlog of ideas and directions** – Let's imagine you're rocking with your three wonderful venues, but one of them seems to have begun to fade. Fewer and fewer comments are made to your column and your book sales have dropped off a bit. What's an author to do? Give it a reasonable amount of time to bounce back, but be honest with yourself. The cash road might have simply played out and its time to move on. Make a graceful exit, wishing them well and step away from the venue. Sometimes you will enjoy the company owners or website manager so much you hate to leave, but your time is money, and it must be spent where it can create new and more sales. For this reason, you must constantly be on the lookout for new and interesting venues. Is there a country steak house chain that might like your idea for their on-line website? How about a sports bar or even a sports team? Are there other on-line businesses connected with country music or cowboy boots? Always heel a list of ideas and directions so that when you have an opening you're ready to shift gears, pitch new venues, and make new fans and book buyers.

- **Test often for success** – Watch your sales, watch the responses to your columns or articles, and watch the responses to your promotions about being at a venue each time you promote it. Watch everything and pay attention to changes, good or bad. Keep a log book. I use a simple lined paper spiral notebook. I note the week, all the venues and promotional efforts I'm doing during the 30 day period, and just make notes. You'll be amazed how much you can learn from doing this. You might discover that Thursday is a terrible day to promote these articles so you promote on Wednesday or Friday for a month to see if things change. Testing is like everything else and too much can be as bad as not enough. Make notes on your activities once each month and give it three months before analyzing the results. It often takes that long for an audience to warm up to a new idea. Besides, if you're doing all your standard marketing, there should be no drop in your sales. The goal of cross marketing is to grow beyond the status quo, and those efforts must be given enough time to bloom and show their colors.

- **Be nice** – Like every other part of life, creating relationships with businesses for a symbiotic success goal can be easy and fun, or very difficult. If you find yourself in a thorny position, be polite and professional. If someone is hard to work with, be careful about how you respond to them and most importantly, how you talk about them on your social networks. NEVER pass on negative opinions or information about a venue. Never complain about them and never do anything to hurt their business. The first rule of thumb is to be careful not to have a contract with them. Keep the relationship informal and friendly and very open ended. Make this an agreement where either party can terminate the relationship at any time for any reason. If you're not locked in, you're not going to feel trapped or uncomfortable. If they can send you packing for any reason, they'll feel more comfortable sitting back and letting you do your thing. Should a relationship end, shake hands with a smile, wish them luck and move on.

When is Too Far, Too Much?

I challenge you to guess what this list represents.

Fallen Too Far
One Note Too Far
A Passage Too Far
Too Far From Reality
Too Far From Home
Too Far For Love
Too Far to Whisper
Never Too Far
Pushed Too Far
A Ridge Too Far
Going Too Far
Stars Too Far
Too Far Gone
Too Far to Go
No Distance Too Far
Too Fast, Too Far

A Race Too Far
Too Far to Rope
A Secret Too Far

Nope, these are not song lyrics or even song titles. They are actually book titles. According to Amazon, at this moment there are 770,343 book titles with the words "Too Far" in the title. I'm taking that as a sign that sometimes too far is just too much. Some of us might need to rethink the title for our next book, unless we want to be number 770,344 on that list.

SLEIGHT OF HAND ASSIGNMENT

Sleight of hand is a trick of illusion, and in an effort to help you feel more comfortable with locating niche and cross markets, and using the platforms of businesses or organizations that talk to those markets, I'm going to create an illusion for you.

Imagine you've written one of the following books:

- *To Kill a Mockingbird*, by Harper Lee
- *Gone with the Wind*, by Margaret Mitchell
- *The Clan of the Cave Bear*, by Jean M. Auel
- *The Hobbit*, by J. R. R. Tolkien
- *The Stand*, by Stephen King
- *The Da Vinci Code*, by Dan Brown
- *Huckleberry Finn*, by Mark Twain
- *Outlander*, by Diana Gabaldon

If you haven't read any of these, choose one you know well and love.

Now sit quietly and imagine the cross and niche markets for the book of your choice. Where are those alternative target markets and how can you reach them? Once you've identified the venues (blogs, businesses on-line and live, clubs and organizations) to help you reach the alternative target markets, what would you pitch to them?

Play your imagination like a piano, shifting from harmony to melody and from single notes to multiple cords. Would law students be a good alternative selling target for To Kill a Mockingbird? Might vintage civil war clothing websites be a great venue for cross marketing Gone with the Wind? Stretch as far as you can and identify three possible directions to go to locate niche or cross markets for your chosen book.

This assignment is a sleight of hand assignment specifically designed to show you how easy it is to locate cross markets and alternative targets for any book. It only seems hard for you because you are so close and emotionally connected with your own book. After completing this assignment, hopefully you understand the simplicity of digging for unique hooks and using them to reach expanded markets for any book … even and most especially, yours.

PART 4
ADVANCED GENRE GAME SKILLS

"The moment you doubt whether you can fly, you cease to ever be able to do it."

~ J.M. Barrie, Peter Pan

USING GENRES TO MARKET

Everyone knows what a genre is, but most authors don't clearly understand what the official genre titles are for, and more specifically, why they exist. The explanation is easy.

It's sort of like going to the grocery store where you automatically know that the cake mix aisle of the store will also have sugar, chocolate chips, shortening, and baking powder. Yes, it's logical and it makes sense, but it's also arranged to make you buy more. If things were randomly set up with the cake mix beside the cans of vegetables which are next to paper plates, there's less chance of luring you into buying more than you had originally planned. The way it's set up now, you may choose to purchase a yellow cake mix, then notice the pineapple pie filling and decide to put that on top of your cake. You're running low on brown sugar, right? Grab that. Oh, and why not pick up some chocolate chips and bake cookies too this week. See? That's how they market to you. The grocery store has just cross marketed you from a plain yellow cake to a pineapple cake and some cookies.

Book stores, both brick and mortar and on-line, do the same thing. If you're looking for a romance book, on the romance section shelves you'll find a number of romance subgenres too. You'll see historic, paranormal, and contemporary romance, all there to hopefully cross market more books. And that's how   they market to you.

Since the first primal book store owner creature placed the first book on the first stone shelf, there have been official, specific genres with subgenres. Aside from attempting to up-sell the book browser from one book to two or three, the book stores also use genre categories to control and determine inventory.

This inventory control system developed by brick and mortar bookstores has more to do with what gets published than you may think. Bookstores drive the traditional publishing industry, not the other way around. The bookstores determine what they will stock based on the analysis of sales in each genre. If the brick and mortar big chains who purchase, inventory, and sell books determine that they no longer want new science fiction books because sales of that particular genre have dropped, they tell the big publishers. The publishers tell the literary agents who back off on accepting science fiction submissions and you, the science fiction author, find yourself facing some interesting challenges.

On-line book stores may see the same drop in science fiction book sales, but they're not concerned with it. On-line bookstores like Amazon have no inventory to deal with and no expense for staff to shelf, rotate stock, or return unsold books. Needless to say, there will always be science fiction to be found.

This is a brief story that I also told in *Finding Author Success*, but it deserves repeating because it clearly explains where I'm going with this.

A few years back, author Danielle Trussoni wrote the novel *Angelology*. She and her literary agent called it a literary work, but after months of getting no positive response from the publishers (most likely because the sales of literary books dropped drastically over the past decade and so bookstores weren't stocking them), the agent decided to play the genre game. Inside the manuscript were powerful adventures, supernatural events, and a curious society of Nephilim (human/angle hybrid creatures). The literary agent decided to take another run at the publishers, this time calling *Angelology* a supernatural horror. This shift in his approach spurred a bidding war that (rumor has it) led to a six figure advance. What this creative and tenacious literary agent did was cross market to gain new and expanded interest in his client's book.

We all know the major genres:

- Romance
- Mystery
- Science fiction/ steampunk
- Historic
- Fantasy

- Women's fiction
- Horror
- Nonfiction, which is not really a genre but for this discussion, we'll include it.

Each primary genre has a plethora of official and unofficial subgenres that create a mish-mash of many of the main genres rolled together.

Genres are categories to benefit those who inventory and shelf books. That's all. Really. There's no bigger reason behind them, even though the publishing industry creates a huge mystery around genre identification and subgenre qualification for querying authors. Most literary agents and publishers have different descriptions for each genre and subgenre category, many can't agree, and the book stores, brick and mortar and on-line, do their own thing when categorizing genres for book display.

Now that you understand who determines genres, why they are so specific, and that sales drive the publishing industry, it's time to shift gears from the industry's use of genres, to using genres as a powerful tool for your cross marketing.

The long standing yet sometimes unclear genre categories have boxed authors into tight pigeonholes and left them to believe that there is only one way to describe their book, and only one target audience for selling their book. Not so. We are free to play the genre game.

Let's imagine you own a beauty salon. Your primary customers will be women seeking a stylist to cut, color, or style their hair. One of those women might bring in her child for an appointment. Now you've found a cross market and a new customer, children, and you stick a sign on your window stating that you style kids hair too. One afternoon, one of your stylists mentions that she does manicures, and you set up a station for her where she can do manicures and pedicures and another sign goes into your window. You've cross marketed further and your customer base just grew again. After that, you put a few shelves up and stocked them with shampoos, conditioners, hair treatments, nail polish, and brushes and combs. Have you gained more customers with the products? Not exactly but you have gained more sales and loyalty from your existing customers.

The point of this hairy example is simple. Cross marketing works on a variety of levels for new exposure, but it also helps with creating stronger ties to your existing fans.

Let's look at another example. Picnics. Last summer I overbooked and went to three different picnics in one day. Picnic number one was easy and fun, a few hot dogs and burgers on the grill, some potato salad, a watermelon, and all the fixings for s'mores. Nice. The next picnic was a small gathering of close foodie friends. They brought delicious cold rosemary dusted, fried chicken, a grilled veggie salad and gourmet oatmeal cookies. After that, I was invited to a romantic dinner picnic for two with grilled lamb chops, a great imported cheese, a crusty loaf of French bread, and a bottle of wine.

In this case we've looked at an extremely broad genre, the picnic genre, and identified the easy, the foodie, and the romantic picnic subgenres.

The picnic and beauty salon examples may seem elementary, but everything about cross marketing is extremely simple. They're going on all the time right under our noses. So many authors become caught up in the publishing rules and regulations universe, they forget to look around. Cross marketing swirls around us all the time.

If mystery is your primary genre, it's just the jumping off point for your cross marketing efforts. Explore deeply in your manuscript to discover how many possible subgenres you can cross market to. Is your mystery a period piece? Does it have a little steampunk flavor? Is there romance involved? Are there paranormal elements in the book like ghosts? Is there a hint of horror in your story?

A yes answer to any of the questions above might cover only a secondary plot to the story, but if so, it is a terrific cross marketing direction. Stretch out your mental minions like curious fingers and comb through your book. If you're marketing to mystery readers, it could be extremely profitable to slip in some marketing to groups that fit the various subgenres you uncover. You shouldn't go to a romance audience and call it a romantic mystery, but you certainly can go to a romance audience and tell them that your book is a mystery with some wonderful romance elements. You might even alter your 25 - 30 word pitch to attract this audience.

Literary agents perfected the genre game for pitching to major publishers. There's no reason we can't use it to help gain more sales for our books. Playing a great genre game is all about understanding the secondary target audiences you're going after. Do your homework. Every book can grow a new and profitable audience simply by flying out of the genre pigeonhole.

The standard genre game is simply a matter of shifting and rolling the various genres and subgenres to create broader targets for marketing a book. Advanced genre game skills create genres on steroids and markets you might have never thought of.

Now it's time to have some fun!

ADVANCED GENRE GAMING FOR CROSS MARKETS

In order for you to play the advanced genre game for cross marketing your book, you need to be playful and creative. Toss the industry standards out the window. Imagine inventing a genre category that perfectly fits your book and exposes the perfect cross and niche markets you should approach. Imagine taking a hurdle over to the bestselling authors' side of the fence by simply laughing and having fun with the potential. It's possible, very easy, and goes something like this.

Start with your primary genre; then add a unique story element. Do it two or three times and see what you come up with. For example:

- Women's fiction/ horsey *(because the main character raises horses)*
- Women's fiction/ inspirational *(because she has overcome a terrible injury)*
- Women's fiction/ green *(because she is careful and respectful with the earth around her)*

Isn't that fun? The point of playing advanced genre games is to take your thinking way beyond the cubbyhole accepted genre concepts. Creating these very specific target market genres helps you identify and expand your cross markets.

What if you went even further? How many more different or expanded audiences could you identify? Now it might be the:

- Women's fiction/ horsey/ riding boots/ feed grain/ stables/ equestrian genre
- Women's fiction/ inspirational/ physical rehabilitation/ prosthetic support groups genre
- Women's fiction/ green/ ecological/ sustainable/ health/ all natural genre

By simply extrapolating your original creative cross market genres, can you see how many new directions you can go with your marketing and promotions? By being creative you've identified all these wonderful unique targeted book buyers and not one of them falls into the standard book marketing strategy every other women's fiction author is using.

This book can easily cross market to equestrian and horse riding groups, cowboy boot stores, green advocates, and even support physical rehabilitation charities. How many other women's fiction authors will be talking to those particular audiences? None. You've just taken yourself away from the competition and tripled your sales through cross marketing. And trust me, nothing is more fun that selling a lot of books.

NOTE: Just a reminder, you'll never use the genre game or advanced genre gaming when pitching your book to or querying for literary agent representation or a publisher. This process of extending genre is designed simply to help you see your extended and alternative markets more clearly and explore new directions for reaching out to more readers and book buyers.

MAKING A GENRE EXPANSION PLAN

By now, you already understand that whatever you want to do with your cross marketing efforts will require a plan. I taught a live workshop recently and the most predominant question among the author students was, "How do I know it will work?" The answer is easy, we don't know these new avenues will pan out, be profitable, or create new sales. Cross Marketing Magic for Authors is all new ground, and bigger than that, it's an all new strategy developed for the author and their book alone. These strategies can't be tested like leavening agents for baking bread, or cleaning products for mopping your floor, and there's a good reason for that. Each and every cross or niche market target is created specifically for one book. The cool unique hooks and elements you wrote into your book are not in other author's books, so no one else is approaching them for book marketing. You are the only one who can find these target markets and in many cases, you will be the first to explore these avenues.

It takes a lot of thought and time to uncover cross and niche markets for your book. No one wants to waste time on a target that isn't quite right, so there are a few strategic questions you should ask before diving into the deep end.

- **Is it real?** In the beginning of this book as we covered the importance of having a perfect 25 word pitch, we talked briefly about writing your 10 word sound bite. I suggested you first write a 10 word sound bite for your favorite book by another author. It was easy, right? Know why? It was easy because you only know the book you read. You don't know what the author hoped you'd to think of the book, what they loved most about the book, what was eliminated from the book, or what never got into the book. All you know is the book. When you're developing your cross marketing targets, always ask the question, "Is it a real cross market, or is it a cross market I wish I could approach?" You are very close to your work and at times it's hard to define the line between what you wish your story told a reader, and what your story really tells them. This is where your friends, editors and readers come in handy. After creating your wonderful extended genre category, run it by those who have read your book. Do they agree that green is a good cross market? Or will they suggest that there isn't enough focus on green living in the story to attract and hold that market? You might be passionate about living a green, sustainable life. You might have a compost pit in your backyard and recycle everything possible. Your main character might do those things too, but is it a strong enough element to be defined as a unique hook for a cross or niche market? Ask your proofreaders, editors, publisher, anyone who has read the book and knows the book in a slightly more distant way than you do. This small effort can save you a lot of time, marketing energy, and frustration.

- **Is it a viable audience?** How many equestrian schools and stables actually exist? My understanding is that there are at least ten in every state in the U.S., and at most, there are as many as a hundred. It's a guess, and certainly not good enough to take this kind of cross marketing leap. Do your homework. If equestrian schools and stables represent a serious unique hook and you discover that there are ten thousand such schools and stables in the English speaking world and a vast number of students train for equestrian riding each year, by all means, begin your plan. This goes for any possible cross or niche market. Be positive it's a viable audience before including it in your strategy, because getting in front of this market requires some time and energy. Be sure you're not wasting that time on target markets that aren't big enough to sell to.

- **Can you do it both live and on-line?** How expansive or narrow is your life? Many authors have gotten into a cyber rut and forgotten that most of life is going on away from the computer. Continuing with the equestrian schools and stables target, I strongly suggest you explore and research even further. What kinds of things attract people within this equestrian culture? Clothing styles for riding apparel? Magazines, newspapers, blogs or Yahoo! Groups that talk about the equestrian life? Are there stores on-line (or down the street) that sell necessities and frivolities to the equestrian culture? What are those items? Charms for their bracelets? Belt buckles? Helmets? Mucking boots? T-shirts that say "Happy Chaps!" Once you've uncovered the depth and width of this particular target cross market, make sure it's strong both live and on-line. For example, can you connect with this audience at equestrian shows? Can you connect with them through guest blogging on blogs about equestrian competitions? Can you connect with them through a supplier company's website with a monthly column? Can you arrange to do a book signing at an equestrian supplies store? In other words, can you reach this audience live *and* on-line, because if it's only one or the other, you may find you have limited yourself. Granted, most businesses, cultures (like horse lovers or licorice lovers or Harley Davidson lovers), and trends can be connected through internet activity, but it's very important to be seen as a living, breathing author too. Never underestimate the power of making yourself accessible to your fans, whether they're basic genre fans, or part of your much broader expanded genre fans.

- **Does it serve you for future books?** Creative solutions can range from simple to multifaceted and complex. It's vital that you determine how far you want to go with a particular target cross market. If you love horses and the equestrian culture, and have plans to either write more books on the subject, or create a series, it is well worth your time and energy to develop close bonds with this target because they will buy your next book and the book after that. On the other hand, if this is the only book you intend to ever write that has this particular unique hook, you may want to keep your efforts clean and simple yet effective: guest blogs, perhaps one or two different websites where you write a column, and at least one book signing at an equestrian event or store. Then you'll be moving on to marketing and cross marketing your next book to its own cross market targets.

- **What is your Planning Strategy?** Once you've done all your research and answered all the questions, you can begin planning. Respect your writing time, be strategic about the target cross markets you will work with, and be consistent. Set your goals. How many more books do you want to sell? How much money do you want to make? How many hours will you dedicate to this cross market? A plan should span no less than three months and no more than twelve months. At the end of each ninety day period, you should take a look at your efforts and determine if it was worth the amount of sales gained. Always tweak your strategies to get the most out of them. For example, if there is a major equestrian competition coming to your town in July, you should create a strategy that builds to and around the event, involves the event and even promotes the event to your readers, fans, followers and friends. Have a contest or free giveaway of a few books along with all the excitement. When it's over, be sure to have follow up strategies like blog reports on the event and everything that impressed you about it. Notice, you're not talking about selling your book. What you are doing here is talking about things the blog reader, friend or follower loves and is also in your book. This creates fans and book buyers far better than shouting that you wrote a book about horses and everyone in ear shot should buy it.

It's a bird! It's a plane!

Advanced genre game skills are so easy even a child can do it. Ask any preschooler what something is. It could be anything, a car, a person a flower or vegetable and you'll be amazed how many different ways that young person will answer.

According to my youngest grandson, a woman can be:

- A lady
- A girl
- A teacher
- A crossing guard
- A doctor
- A nurse
- A dentist
- A grandmother
- A stranger
- A pretty lady
- A mean lady
- A nice lady

Now, if you look at this list and imagine that your genre is romance and your primary target is women, how many niche or cross markets can you locate in this child's description list? You can market to older women and younger women if the story is appropriate. You can reach out to groups of teachers or nurses or policewomen because female crossing guards like romance just like any other woman. You can speak with groups of women who gather for special interests

---

like gardening, neighborhood safety, or community service.

It's a very simple genre extrapolation skill that you, even though your far older than a toddler, should keep alive and in practice. Let your mind be like a child's when playing the genre game.

SUPERNATURAL ASSIGNMENT

I challenge you to dig as deep as possible into your manuscript and uncover every single unique hook you have in the story. To identify your unique hooks, remember that it must relate to a primary character or location, and it must be consistent throughout the story.

For example, your usually focused and supportive fantasy creature sidekick (think Chewbacca) can only be calmed after battle if he's fed sugar. In this case sugar and sugar related products are a unique story element. Sugar and sugar related products are also a possible cross market direction.

If your book takes place at the seashore, all things of the sea and sea shore culture are unique hooks. But if sugar or the sea shore are only mentioned once or twice in the book, they are not strong enough unique hooks and should not be part of your SUPER Genre.

Now that you've found your unique hooks, extend your genre to an amazing twenty plus word SUPER Genre. It might look something like this:

Fantasy/ romance/ mystery/ twins/ island /ancient weapons/ sailing ships/ seafood/ military training/ war/ racism/ politics/ magic/ witchcraft/ ancient gods/ mystics/natural healing/ herbs/ old world trade/ spies/ mercenaries

From this massive twenty plus word SUPER Genre, you can easily see as many as five or six completely new and original directions to go for your cross marketing efforts. You can reach out to antique weapons aficionados through related subject bloggers who have those followers. You can have fun with ships, or ship lovers. You can connect with new age stores and on-line websites selling herbs and natural remedies.

Create a twenty plus word SUPER Genre for your current book, your past books, and your future books. There are undiscovered cross markets in those SUPER Genres to help revive sales for your back list. There are ways to write cross markets into future books without compromising the story, so be sure to think about SUPER Genres when you're plotting or imagining your next project.

There are so many possibilities when you put everything in a long line of key words. While all the other fantasy writers are shouting to fantasy fan clubs and hash marking the word fantasy to death, you're talking to a completely different book buyer. SUPER indeed!

PART 5
APPROACHING AND MAINTAINING CROSS MARKETS

"The voyage of discovery is not in seeking new landscapes but in having new eyes."

~ Marcel Proust

DO YOUR HOMEWORK

Long ago, we sat in elementary school and scribbled our assignment into our workbook with a dull number two lead pencil. Little did any of us know, that exercise would continue throughout our entire lives. Since those formidable years, we've read history books to make reports, studied math and science, researched colleges and universities, then started the whole process over again. Back then, our goal was to graduate and end all the study. Go figure.

As employees we study employee manuals, rules and regulations, product or service parameters and appropriate behavior. If we're entrepreneurial by nature, we start a business and study the laws and regulations for everything from product storage, employee liability, the IRS, and the priority of growing sales. Our goal is to make a living, perhaps even become very successful.

One of the toughest jobs I have is convincing authors that they are, in fact, entrepreneurs, whether they're self-published or published by one of the big publishing houses. Everything about an author's life involves creating exposure and sales for their books. An author who doesn't think this is true isn't an author for long. They lose their publishing contracts, or realize that being published means nothing if no one buys or reads their book.

If you are an author, you are in business and what do business people do? Homework. The first things you must determine are exactly what you want, and how to get it.

- Fans
- Book sales
- Demand for your next book
- Money
- Success
- The respect of your peers

In the case of basic marketing, you learn the social networks, how to use them, how to populate them with prospective book buyers, and how to keep those friends, fans, and followers faithful to you and your books. You create awareness, implement powerful promotions and create strong relationships with the media.

For advanced marketing strategies like niche and cross marketing, you need to have a clear grasp of the basics then run a little wild. Even with that running wild fun, there are rules.

You must take the time and be dedicated enough to not only find your extensive SUPER Genres, but discover which of those many and varied genre descriptions can serve as a viable cross market. Your contemporary romance might have a mortician in it, but are funeral homes and embalmers a viable potential book buyer market? Only you can decide. If your mortician loves Italian food and eats at Italian restaurants every chance he gets, Italian restaurants and Italian food stores might be great venues for readings and book signings. Bloggers about Italian food might be a great place to connect with Italian food lovers. Connecting with a local Italian chef might add to some of your cross marketing efforts, especially if he shares a recipe with you for your blog, or is willing to support a charity your book is supporting.

Always remember, just because one of your SUPER Genre cross markets is cool and interesting, doesn't always mean it's a feasible direction to go. If one of your unique hooks is a Komodo dragon, and your research uncovers that fact that only three zoos in America have a Komodo dragon in captivity and your local zoo isn't one of them, using the Komodo dragon as a unique hook and throwing a launch party at your local zoo would not be a good idea. However, if your research uncovers not only the fact that your local zoo has several Komodo dragons, but also every other zoo in America has Komodo dragons and there is an actual Komodo dragon fan club of exotic animal lovers, you just might have hit the jackpot. There might be a huge possible following for your particular unique hook.

The power of a unique hook isn't necessarily that it is unique to your book and story, as much as the fact that it is a unique marketing direction with a substantial following. Chocolate, coffee, amusement parks, antique cars, tattoos, and Harley Davison bikes represent obvious huge sales targets. Uncovering an untapped huge sales target based on your unique hook, like Komodo dragons or equestrian competition fans, can be even more rewarding.

Be sure to connect with markets that represent enough sales potential for your book. You might love a concept, but without a market for it, you will be wasting a lot of time.

CROSS MARKET APPROACHES AND PROPOSALS

There are as many ways to approach a cross market as there are to approach a regular market. You can advertise to them. You can friend them on Facebook and Twitter. You can target all your blog subject matter (and your important SEO tags) toward them. You can make friends with them by joining their Facebook, Twitter or Yahoo! Groups. You can do all the things you do when you're reaching out to your direct genre lovers, the only difference is that there are no other authors shouting to drown you out, so you have the whole cross market pretty much to yourself. Like that idea? Of course you do. But because cross markets are not used to being approached by authors, there are a few subtle and savvy ways to make your approaches, no matter how simple or complex your plan might be.

You've done all your research and you know the chosen cross market is loaded with potential book buyers because it is strong with people interested in your unique hook. For these examples, let's imagine your unique hook is one of the biggies, coffee. Your main character owns a coffee shop where people meet face-to-face for the first time after chatting on an on-line dating website. The book title is Coffee with Love and a Shot of Murder. How do you approach this romance/ murder mystery/ coffee lovers SUPER Genre target audience?

- **Social Networks** – Because you understand basic marketing strategies, you are already using Twitter and Facebook to reach lovers of romance and mysteries. This is how you cross market to your unique hook target.
    - o **Twitter.** To begin cross marketing to this unique hook target, you will locate coffee lovers on Twitter by searching the word coffee and through hash tags like #coffee, #cafe, #cappuccino, and #espresso. As the flow of coffee related tweets feed past, read through them. Is the tweeter a person talking about how much they love coffee or a specific café or perhaps specialty

coffee drinks like a vanilla latte or iced mocha? That person is a good one to follow. Continue this process for about 10 minutes each day for a week and you'll find you have followed quite a few people. Many of those people will follow you back, provided you have something in your bio or description that states your book title and basic 25 word pitch. Once you have amassed a good number of coffee lover followers, you're ready to market to them and use Twitter effectively.

- ○ **Facebook** is just as easy, but in ways that are a little more subtle. For one thing, Facebook greatly limits your ability to build friends at a fast pace, giving you the equivalent of a time-out if you try to build your friend base too quickly. I strongly suggest you make friends a slightly different way to get around this Facebook limitation. First of all, search out coffee lovers groups, cafés, and other groups related to coffee drinks. Examine the posts and the other friends posting there, and if it fits your target prospective book buyer, join. Once you join you will have access to their friends list. You can't just friend them all without getting your wrist slapped, but you can be social in the group, then simply post and ask them to friend you at your Facebook page. See, easy. You can do the same on Twitter by inviting your fellow coffee lovers over to your Facebook page for a cup of coffee and some fun. Once you've made good coffee friends in strong numbers on Facebook and Twitter, you can begin to communicate with them. You can share a coffee fact each day on Facebook and Twitter. Be sure to end your Facebook coffee fact with an open ended question to encourage response. Pop in every few hours and reply to responses, even if it's just to hit the "like" button for a comment. Remember to twist something about your book into these daily facts. Be creative, have fun, occasionally post your book cover and book's buy link, send Twitter followers and Facebook friends to your website and blog, and constantly be on the lookout for more target market friends and followers to pull into your networks.

- **Blogs** – There has been a lot of talk lately about blogs being a useless waste of time for selling books, and for the most part I agree. If an author blogs to other authors talking about the process of writing or selling a book, it will not sell books. If an author creates a blog expecting prospective book buyers and fans to flock around just to see what they will say next, again, few to no sales are being made. There's an effective and efficient way to use blogging as a powerful marketing and cross marketing tool, but it takes creative thought and reaching out to the right target audiences.

o **Your blog.** Just as the subject of your tweets and Facebook posts is coffee, your blogs too should reach out to coffee lovers and attract them to your book. Blogging has an additional power punch in that the search engines pick up not only your content and title, but your strategically chosen tag words. Create a series of six blogs to be posted every other week that are themed for coffee love around the world. Each blog might focus on the country a specific coffee bean comes from, and something romantic about that country. At the end of each blog, you will insert a picture of your book cover and the buy link. Now you're on your way to sales success. Your blog entry isn't the same old tired drivel about writing or free book promotions or begging your blog followers to bring friends or join your street team. Instead it's targeted to a new, broad audience and it reads like an interesting article about coffee instead of a desperate author trying to sell books. Your title should contain the word coffee along with elements of romance or murder in it. Your SEO tags should include coffee, romance, murder mystery, your name, the book title, and something directly related to the subject of the blog post, like Arabica coffee beans, or Columbian coffee. Anyone searching coffee information or coffee entertainment will find your blog. If they enjoy it, they will become a blog follower, and if they continue to love what you tell them about coffee, they will buy your book and become a fan.

o **Other blogger's blogs.** Another powerful blogging tool is someone else's blog. No, not another author's blog. Too many authors spend far too much time guest blogging on each other's blogs. All they are really doing is filling in for the author who doesn't want to blog that week. They are talking to the other author's fans and it's unlikely to sell a book at all. What I mean when I suggest using someone else's blog is different than   you might think. Google coffee blogs and look at all the people who blog about coffee. www.coffeesage.com lists hundreds of coffee blog categories and pages. Some are coffee companies, some are coffee distributors, but most are normal, everyday people who just love coffee. All are great places to approach and ask to guest blog. These bloggers already have a solid following of coffee lovers, exactly what you're looking for. We'll explore how to create relationships with these blog owners in the next section.

- **Organizations** – There are national and international coffee organizations. Will any of them be a good place to cross market? Only digging into the organization structure will answer that question. They may have an organization-wide employee or outreach newsletter in which you can buy an ad. They might be interested in supporting books about coffee or fiction where coffee is a unique hook. They may like an author to post a monthly coffee and reading tip for their employees. It's all great, especially if they let you show your book cover and buy link at the end of your little article or tip.

- **Clubs and Groups** – There are coffee of the month clubs. Will they be interested in purchasing books from you to include in their gift package? Yahoo! lists 8,347 groups with the word coffee in their title. There are sure to be at least a hundred with a large number of members that focus on coffee and loving coffee. These coffee aficionados get together and talk about coffee. Join a few groups, make friends, talk about coffee and never, ever ask anyone to buy your book. Instead make sure your book title, 25 word pitch, and buy link is in your email signature. Occasionally ask for information about a special kind of coffee for your blog or as research for your next book. If you've made friends and been supportive and involved, members will ask about your books and buy your books simply because you didn't show up and beg for a sale. In addition to on-line activity, it's very likely you can find a local coffee lovers group that meets every month or so at a coffee shop or café. Reach out and offer to do a reading and book signing at one of their meetings.

- **On-line Businesses** – Who sells coffee or coffee makers on-line? Everyone from Starbucks to Gevalia and Green Mountain, as well as Keurig and Mr. Coffee. How can you creatively connect with them? The *Caffeine Murder Tip of the Week*? A *Romancing the Bean* monthly column? A deal on books for them to put into their gift baskets? Brief videos where you talk about coffee and do a reading from your book? The ball's in your court because authors never approach these businesses for symbiotic sales connections.

- **Live Businesses** – Most authors forget to look right in their own home town for cross marketing opportunities. Ask local coffee shops and cafés to sell your book on their shelves along with those pretty coffee mugs and travel mugs. Ask local gift basket stores and florists to consider including your book in their packages. Schedule readings and speaking engagements and book signings in coffee shops, in a department store home goods section next to the coffee makers, or at high-end gourmet grocery stores. Every time and every place you connect with one of your cross markets, you have a strong opportunity to sell books. Why? Because no one else is there trying to sell them books. It's new to them and always a win/win situation. The business, group, or organization isn't losing money by letting you connect with their customer. In fact, they have a good shot at gaining new customers from your fan base because you'll be letting everyone know where you are and what you're doing through your blogs, Twitter, and Facebook activity.

PERFECT YOUR QUERY

Do you remember sending out queries to find literary agent representation or publication? Perhaps you still send queries for those reasons. Most likely you're at the level where you're querying for other things too, like reviews, event participation, speaking engagements, or to ask venues for reading and book signing opportunities. No matter what you query for, your query is the tool for getting past a gate keeper. If you queried agents and publishers, when you received a rejection it was not for your book, it was a rejection of your query. The same is true when you query for other reasons. Your pitch wasn't clear enough, your letter wasn't organized or powerful enough, or you contacted the wrong person altogether. Authors deal with rejection every day, there's no need to ask for more.

Contacting a venue for your cross marketing efforts is no different than querying a publisher. The query is a business communication where you are asking for something specific. If you effectively follow these six tips, you will find more success than failure.

- **Find the correct contact.** If you were querying a literary agency, you'd study each of the agents, which genres they represent, and even go as far as learn how many of the authors represented by that agent have been published before choosing to query them. Locating the correct contact for your cross marketing efforts is the same, yet a little different. The difference is that these are businesses or bloggers who have a goal in mind that has nothing to do with you. A literary agent sees you as a way to earn a better living. If they sell your book to a publisher, they make a commission and ongoing royalties. It's a clear win/win scenario. But when you reach out to a cross market venue, it's not such a clear win/win for the person you're contacting, so it's your job to sell your idea. Needless to say, locating and reaching out to the correct contact is important.

  - **Blogs** – If your book is about a murder at a lighthouse and the story is set in the early 1900's, you might consider approaching bloggers who focus on lighthouses, lighthouse maintenance, lighthouse history, Victorian lifestyle, or vintage and Victorian fashion. If you look carefully at the blog, search every tab and link, you might easily locate the owner of the blog and an email address for them. If it's not there, you can simply comment on one of the blog entries and state that you have an idea for a guest blog and would like to speak with the blog's owner. Most will respond positively.

  - **Company websites** – If your unique story hook is scuba diving and you wish to connect with scuba diving supply company websites, there are a few things to do. Research the company and make sure it's been around a while. Be sure to explore the entire website and see if they are currently doing anything like what you plan to propose. For example, if you want to propose a monthly tropical adventure report, it's wise to be sure they aren't already doing an adventure report. The next thing to do is seek out the website contact information. If there is a marketing or promotions manager listed, that's the perfect contact. If there is only a webmaster listed so that viewers can report web issues, locate the company phone number and request the name and contact information for the website marketing or promotions manager. Having a name is far more powerful than simply sending an email or letter to *Dear Marketing Manager*. It speaks of your professionalism and gains valuable brownie points.

- o **Company locations** – Suppose you want to hold a book launch event for *Tropical Murder* at a scuba supply store. This one is even easier. Naturally, you will need to visit several local scuba supply stores to examine their location, how creative, neat and fun their store is, how the floor plan is laid out and if they are doing promotions of any kind. They might have guest speakers who talk about different scuba locations in the world. Perhaps they host monthly scuba club meeting. A spokesperson from the product manufacturers might be scheduled to speak and explain product improvement to the store's customers. If the scuba supply store does these types of things, they're likely to be very open in your idea. If not, it might be a slightly harder sell. Your goal is to discover who makes the marketing or promotional event decisions. Talk with the store manager. He might be the man, but if the store is a chain or owned by a different corporation, you will need to ask the manager for contact names. Be sure to get him excited about your proposal. That way when you connect with the right person, they will have already heard about your book launch event idea.

- **Open with your request.** Most queries are the same, whether the local police ask you to support their charities, or the gas company requests your input on their annual service survey. The biggest mistake authors make when writing queries is beating around the bush and getting to the point too slowly. These are business people or blog owners. Most are not interested in your back story, how you became an author, the inspiration behind your book, or even your 25 word pitch right up front. First they want to know what you want; then they might be interested in more. Get to the point quickly. "Dear Mister Smith, I would like to propose a monthly column on your website that is sure to create regular visits by coffee lovers." In those few words you've perked his ears because to said a few very strategic things. You told him what you would like to do, and you explained that if you do this, it will bring his website more regular visits and possibly sell more of his product. After that you can explain what qualifies you to write these monthly columns, what ideas you have for the columns, and that all you request in return is an opportunity to note your bio as an author, your book title, and buy link at the end of each column.

- **Explain your plan.** If you are proposing a monthly column or article, suggest titles for the first six months. If it's a flavor of the month article, suggest that you will create content for flavors they choose each month. Tell them how entertaining each article will be and how it will connect with the light side of coffee lovers. If you want to guest blog, don't ask for a one time opportunity, offer to do a fun three part series of blogs on how coffee and love create deadly romantic energy. There's no need to give detailed plans or offer already written sample pieces, just entice the contact with your idea and make him see how connected your suggestion is with his customers. At this point, you may want to offer him an ebook copy of your book. That way he can determine that you are in fact a very good writer and he should consider your proposal.

- **Close with your 25 word pitch.** After you've explained what you are asking for, how you propose to do it, and that your idea is a strong win/win opportunity for both you and the coffee company or blogger, you then (and only then) close your query letter with your 25 word pitch as a final kick.

- **Set expectations.** If your query is powerful and clear, the contact will ask for your proposal.
  - In that proposal you will suggest the timing of your articles or columns. You may state that you will provide a 2,000 word column on the 25th of each month to be posted live on the company's website by the 1st of the next month. That way you will know when to promote it and the webmaster will have time to integrate it into his updating activities.
  - Your proposal should also cover exclusivity of content. Be careful not to offer the company or blogger exclusivity of YOU, only the specific content. Remember, in some cases you might be doing this kind of cross marketing with as many as three businesses and three bloggers. You will guarantee not only exclusivity of content to these companies and bloggers, but exclusivity of concept. For example, one coffee company might have a *Bean of the Month* monthly article, another might have a monthly *Mug 'o Love* column that explores love and coffee in playful ways, and a third company might simply place a copy of

your book into their coffee gift baskets. You will do the same exclusivity of content with bloggers by carefully creating a unique three part series for each blogger and their followers.

o Never ask for or accept payment from or an employee status with a cross marketing venue company. Instead, just obtain permission to subtly promote your book with the title and buy link at the end of each column or article. If they insist on giving you more, ask them for permission to post your book cover at the bottom of your articles. If they still persist, ask them to give you a free ad for your book somewhere on the website in trade for your articles. Always protect your freedom to move on and reach out to more and different prospective book buyers within any target audience.

o The final part of your proposal should include a suggested length of time for the proposed effort. You might suggest a six month commitment with an evaluation after three months. Never offer to sign a contract, but you can create or suggest a very loose agreement with an easy fifteen day out clause. Some venues might love you so much, they never want you to leave, others might find the articles are not benefiting them at all and wish you gone. Chemistry and creativity is the key to success. If a venue is willing to work with you, change the location of your article from one section of the website to another more highly visible section, things could start to click and create sales for you and the company. If they are not willing to help you gain higher visibility with their existing customers, with a fifteen day notice you are free to go to another company that may be much more effective.

- **Be patient.** After making your proposal, don't expect an immediate integration into their website or blog. Some companies work through committees and must pass proposals up to the final decision makers. Like literary agents or publishers where your book is finally chosen based on a committee decision, many businesses work the same way. It might take time to get started. Don't waste that time, move ahead and continue researching, contacting, and making proposals to other companies and bloggers. It's a first come first serve world, and it's to your advantage. Have a strong list of prospective websites and bloggers and use them. When one falls through, pitch another one. When you have three active venues, keep your eyes peeled for more so that you are always ready to move from a slowing venue to a new, more active one.

CROSS MARKETING WITH PUBLICITY

Publicity is the use of the media to get your message out to the public, but it's far more than that. Publicity is all about tapping into the emotions to create broader awareness of a product or service.

If your neighborhood trash collector recycles in a more eco-friendly way than his competitors and never tells anyone, nothing happens. If he advertises the fact on his trucks, only those awake when he picks up the trash know his news. But if he informs the media through a press release and a few stories are written about his eco-friendly efforts, something much bigger happens. Through the media, newspaper, radio, or television stories, he has tapped into the emotions of people who care about the environment. It's news because his competitors aren't doing it. It's a good story because he's serving his customers as well as protecting the earth. It's interesting because it could easily spur an exploration of how his competitors recycle and why their process is less eco-friendly. Your trash collector has just become more respected in the community and gained more customers who care about eco-friendly recycling. He has cross marketed through publicity and grown his clientele.

To do this for your book, we need to return to SUPER Genres, this time focusing your SUPER Genre efforts on possible charitable services or organizations that might represent strong cross markets. Remember this expanded genre exercise?

- Women's fiction/ horsey (because the main character raises horses)
- Women's fiction/ inspirational (because she has overcome a terrible injury)
- Women's fiction/ green (because she is careful and respectful with the earth around her)
- When we created the SUPER Genres, these two appeared:
- Women's fiction/ inspirational/ physical rehabilitation/ prosthetic support groups genre
- Women's fiction/ green/ ecological/ sustainable/ health/ all natural genre

What we see here are two expanded SUPER Genre descriptions that might open a few powerful cross marketing publicity doors for the author. If you find yourself in this position, explore each possible charity. Which is the biggest and most visible? Which one needs more help? Which one connects most solidly to your book and its unique hook? You must choose just one, so choose carefully. There are three ways an author can cross market with publicity.

- **Donating a portion of book sales to your target charity** – This one is very easy. Let's imagine that you have chosen to support a charity that offers physical rehabilitation at little to no cost to the needy patient. It feels good and right to you so you look deeper into the charity. Locate the donation coordinator and inform them that you would like to donate a portion of your book sales to the charity. To do this you will make sure it is announced on the back cover and inside of your book, on your website, and to your Twitter and Facebook following as well as occasionally blogging about the charity and why you feel strongly about supporting it. Sometimes this is so well received by the charity that they announce it in their newsletter along with an author interview and is a nice boost for your book. Make sure you send a press release out about your support of the charity, your reason for it and how it ties in with your book.

- **Actively participating in the charity's fundraising efforts** – If you create a tight and friendly relationship with your contact at the charity, they will inform you of various events going on to support it. Some will be local and easy to personally participate in, but others might require some outreach on your part. If the charity is doing a big promotional fundraiser with a local sports team, and they are going to have a Chinese auction and/or gift baskets for people to bid on, you might want to donate books for those baskets or a series of your books for a Chinese auction. You may also want to volunteer your time to help with the event. If the event is too far away, you might offer to help promote it among your fans and followers, as well as donate books for their efforts.

- **Creating an event specifically to raise donations and awareness for the chosen charity** – This one is more complex but far more rewarding. You can create an entire event designed to raise donations for your chosen charity. You might hold the event at a riding stable or equestrian school. Invite athletes from all parts of the local athletic world to participate. Pull together assistants from the charity to help you organize and get the event going. Do a press release campaign that announces the charity event named for your book title, and follow up with press releases as local celebrities and athletes join in on the effort. Both you and the charity will actively promote the event. Remember, this direction is very time consuming and will take as many as six months to plan and execute well. On the other hand, the publicity gained could sell thousands of your books, just by your association with such a good and worthy cause.

THE NUANCE OF CROSS MARKETING PROMOTIONS

The hardest thing for an author to do is push their own books, and the second hardest thing for an author to do is NOT to push their books. In all effective cross marketing efforts, pushing is an absolute no-no. Think of it as visiting a strange and foreign land. There are benefits to be had while residing in that wonderful place, but it is THEIR place and making waves is never a good idea. If an author joins a Yahoo! Group for coffee lovers, convinces a scuba shop website to let her write a monthly article, or creates a connection with a blogger who focuses on equestrian culture, it's a good thing. But, if all the author does is talk about their book and where to buy it, nothing productive will happen.

These groups, businesses, and blog communities are focused on their interest, not your book. The nuance of promoting to them is to be one of them. Talk about coffee or scuba diving or horse culture and keep your book as a secondary little footnote at the bottom of all your articles, blogs, tweets, and group emails. Don't make these people feel used and abused. You will benefit far more by being subtle than pushing hard.

Cross marketing targets might take a little longer to warm up to you or they might instantly show results. If you do see a big jump in sales, don't change anything. Remember to inform them when you are involved in or establishing a charity event that relates to your book. If it's a book about riding and you're talking to an equestrian club, they will relate and want to participate. If it's a scuba group and you've discovered a charity that uses scuba diving to connect with autistic individuals, tell them, they will be interested.

The trick to successful cross marketing is to be a person, not an author trying to sell books. The roots you plant within these groups and targets could last forever and they could easily be part of your biggest core fan base. You just need to be patient.

KNOW WHEN TO WALK AWAY

We all know the lyrics to Kenny Rogers' *The Gambler*, but knowing when to walk away can be a little tricky. If you've been working with a coffee company and writing a monthly fun article for their website, be sure to keep notes on all your activity.

If you started in November and didn't pick up steam and sales until February, then you discover that the next November it's a little quiet too, that doesn't mean it's time to walk away. That simply means it's a down cycle for that particular business or industry. Instead of packing up and moving on, add another venue to your efforts, one that is active between November and February, perhaps something like gift baskets. Connect with a gift basket company and propose that they create a *Coffee & Great Reading Gift Basket* for the holidays. Offer to promote it on your website and to your fans and followers. The gift basket company buys your books and promotes it when they market the basket. Always offer a discount for things like this. Talk to your publisher and see what they can arrange.

Some venues are worth riding the low tides because the product or company is growing, and that means they are gaining more and more customers that you can sell your books to.

There's a completely different scenario that might develop. Let's imagine you've connected with a scuba diving company and do monthly articles for their website. These people adore you and will do anything for you. They offer in-store promotional opportunities and have shifted your article placement from inside the website to the very first page. They talk to you all the time on the phone and you even socialize with some of the managers. You love these guys as much as they love you. There's only one problem. This particular venue is not selling books for you.

Before doing anything, make sure you haven't gotten lazy. Have you been blogging about your articles? Reaching out to more and more scuba related friends and followers? Have you been creative with your articles? Have you built your exposure by asking the scuba customers to follow you on Twitter and friend you on Facebook? Consistency is the name of the marketing game, whether you're doing standard marketing or advanced marketing.

If, in fact, you haven't dropped your end of the bargain, take a serious look   at the company. Have they forgotten to tell their customers about your articles? Neglected to promote them in their newsletter or on their social networking? Or worse yet, are they doing badly and struggling to, ahem, stay above water? There are a lot of things to consider when you choose to walk away from a cross marketing effort, but only one tiny thing matters in the decision. The bottom line. Without growing your sales, you are only wasting your time. Know when to walk away.

REPRODUCE SUCCESS

Wow! You sold over 10,000 books in one year through a combination of standard marketing and advanced cross marketing efforts. This is more than double the number of books you sold the year before, when you didn't even know about cross marketing. It proves that commitment and consistency works. It shows that reaching out with SUPER Genres to lovers of your unique hooks, speaking only to prospective book buyers and fans, and connecting with your charity made a major impact. So, now what?

It's important to record everything you can. Take a notebook and create a segment for each of your different cross marketing efforts. Jot down anything and everything you think might have an impact on the bottom line. Did the coffee website go down for a whole week in September due to some technical glitch? Put it in your records. Did you add another venue two months after your first cross marketing venue became active? Make note of that. Did you take a week of vacation in August and ignore your daily social networking responsibilities? Put it in your notes. Did you release a new book with the same unique hooks, making it easy to use the same cross markets? Write it down. Did you release a new book that had nothing to do with your current cross markets? Record the dates.

Then take it a step further. Be sure to make a monthly record of your own activities and how you are managing them. Are you overworked? Tired all the time? Or are you doing just fine and dandy? Enjoying the ride? Be honest and write it all down. Did you see a massive drop in sales in January? Was that drop also reflected for the businesses you are cross marketing with during January? Make a clear note of this, it might be a month when you can take a break, regroup, analyze, and start fresh in February. Everyone needs a break sometime, don't run yourself down. The point of all this is to create sales and build a huge fan base. REMEMBER, once you reach a certain level of sales and exposure, your fans become the most powerful tools for your marketing. This is not going to go on forever. Eventually it will require less and less marketing effort to get a new book to high sales volumes. For now, you're just building.

In the meantime, once every year, perhaps in January when the holidays have died down and everyone quiets for a winter moment, you will need to take that notebook and read it cover to cover. If you've done this correctly, it will show sales and activity cycles for both your book and the various businesses and bloggers you're associated with. This collection of data will clearly expose the successful venues and the duds. It will help you shift your efforts and overlap them more effectively. If your charity does an annual national fundraiser in March, and one of your unique hook cross market venues has a sales surge in March but your book sales always seem to dip a little in March, it might be time to push harder in March to take advantage of the possible publicity and marketing exposure available to you. If your chosen charity needs money in July and your book sales kick butt in July, it might be a wise idea to create a fundraiser to benefit the charity and involve your various other venues and fans during that month.

The only way to reproduce success if to understand what created sales success for you and what didn't. Rome wasn't built in a day, but when it was at its height, Rome was the whole known world. Just don't ever forget that Rome fell and fell hard. Don't let the empire you're building become forgotten until it rots and dies. Keep good notes and learn from your past successes and failures.

MYSTICS OF LONGEVITY ASSIGNMENT

With commitment and consistency, your bottom line will show that there are great advantages to approaching cross markets, but there are even greater reasons for maintaining and growing them, especially if they will serve you in the future. If you write collection or series books that draw from the same cross markets, you have a fantastic opportunity to build and grow those cross markets for your coming books and sales.

If you write freestanding books with vastly varying subject matter and sales targets, maintaining cross marketing efforts will look a little different. Continuing to build a following in a particular cross market can keep the sales of your book profitable, even when it becomes part of your backlist. You must decide how large you want the sales for that book to be, and at what point you're willing to walk away from the cross market.

Either way, growing sales with cross marketing efforts can seriously impact your pocket book, so understanding the process is important.

For this assignment, first we'll imagine you are writing a book series, and then we'll imagine you're writing a stand-alone book.

Let's say you are writing a contemporary mystery/romance series that takes place in Phoenix, Arizona and the primary cross market is country western music. I will leave it to your imagination what the other SUPER Genre titles might be. Let's suppose that with the first book in the series, you used standard marketing strategies and sold 400 books in the first three months of your launch. For your second book launch, you added cross marketing strategies and sold more than 5,000 books over the first three months. The trick is to not only maintain those fans, but to grow them into a larger fan and prospective book buyer base for future books in the series.

To do this assignment, list all the possible cross marketing efforts you will create and have already implemented for this series. Create many new directions and strategies within your SUPER Genre listings to give you a constant stream of growth all the way through to the tenth and final book of this contemporary mystery/romance series. What else do country music lovers like? Horses? Cowboy hats and boots? Rodeos? What are the secondary unique elements in the book? Raising cattle? Running a town? Is the main character an elementary school teacher who falls in love with a country music backup singer at a sports bar? Would that attract prospective book buyers from sports fans? Beer drinkers? School teachers? Be sure to use cross market targets that will respond to the powerful unique hooks consistent in this series, and imagine all the new and additional directions you can go to sell it.

Now shift gears and imagine you wrote a stand-alone women's fiction novel about how a character, who is dedicated to helping the homeless, becomes homeless and manages to pull herself from the depth of despair and into a life even more committed to helping those in such dire situations. What cross markets and publicity directions will you approach? How many prospective book buying targets can you find in this story and what strategies will you use to keep the book front and center for the public and future fans? How will you keep the book's message alive? Annual promotions to create awareness for the plight of the homeless? Ongoing engagements where you travel and speak on the subject? How far can you go, for how long, and what would your final sales goal be for this free standing piece of fiction?

Carefully plot your outlined plans for both the series cross marketing approaches, and the stand alone cross marketing approaches. These can very easily serve as the bones of your own strategies for maintaining and growing your cross markets.

PART 6
EVALUATE, EVALUATE, EVALUATE

"Never stop listening to your audience."

~ David Copperfield

How many marketing, promotional, or gimmicky advertising concepts catch your interest in any given week? How often have you heard a crazy concept and wondered how it could possibly work? You're a smart person, smart enough to see right through some of the silly, illogical, self-indulgent, and impractical concepts that fly across your computer screen daily. If it looks ridiculous, it is. If it seems like it's designed to make a ton of money or create visibility for a party other than you, it is. If it's a concept loaded with other authors, well, I shouldn't have to even mention what a waste of your time it will be.

Granted, a few of these concepts might deserve some of your attention. Ask all the questions and consider the possibilities but always remember, if it landed in your email inbox, it landed in every other author's email inbox too. Why do we even consider these author mass promotional ideas?

I often think of authors as a bunch of frightened writers huddling together and moving like a massive centipede from one marketing idea to another. No one author gets much, but they all get to commiserate together about how difficult it is to market their books.

Avoiding the centipede mentality is the first key to creating success, and cross marketing is one of the most powerful advance marketing tools an author has in their arsenal. Done well, it can change the whole game. Dedication to the system also means keeping a close eye on your trajectory and growing success.

I've worked with authors for years and my favorite question from them has always been, "How will I know if it worked?" At first I thought these people were making a joke, but then I realized that this isn't second nature to authors. Authors aren't used to the systems involved in testing marketing, advertising, or promotional efficiency. So, when the bottom line improves, how can you tell if a specific effort is the reason your sales spiked or not? How will you know if it worked?

Because the author centipede mentality is so prevalent, most authors are, at any given moment, trying any number of crazy marketing activities. They might be doing a free book promotion, a blog tour, running ads in several venues, running a contest, and doing an email campaign all at the same time. If they sell thirty percent more books one week, ten percent fewer the week after that, no books the week after that, then suddenly have a huge fifty percent hike in the fourth week, how on earth can they know what worked and what didn't? There is a way to uncover that information.

The best way to understand your sales results is to systematically implement and test your activity. Needless to say, there will be no other authors shuffling at your side while you do this. No one will be shouting about the newest, coolest promotion in the world and insisting you try it too. It will be much easier to focus, get your message across to book buyers, and understand your results.

There are five wonderful tools for testing your marketing, promotional, and advertising results, but the most important thing to know is that you should not run more than two promotions at a time. Timing is everything, and understanding which promotions to run concurrently is a skill you should perfect. A good rule of thumb is to be sure that the two promotions are targeted at two completely different audiences. For example, using the Victorian mystery book about a murder at a lighthouse, you can do one promotion targeted toward lighthouse lovers and a second promotion focused on Victorian vintage clothing enthusiasts. There can be any number of activities within each promotion, but they will be specific to the cross market target book buyer. You should give a promotion three months from beginning to end. All promotional activity must be planned and the strategy should be documented so that you can follow the plan perfectly, then make notes for future reference.

To test your results you must be honest and fair. If you ran a promotion targeted at football fans during basketball's March Madness, you planned badly and will not see much in the way of usable results for gauging the success or failure of your promotion. By the same token, if you love a particular marketing idea or cross marketing audience and the results are poor, you might need to shrug it off and move past that idea. Simply wanting a promotion to work is not a guarantee that it will work.

I'd like to make a note about testing and building your success. After you've done all the testing and you know that strategy #1 works with one audience and strategy #2 works perfectly with a second audience, you can then run as many different promotions at a time as you'd like. You already know these promotions are effective, so there's no worry about testing them. You can simply increase your sales and fan base with them. Testing in this fashion is vital when you're trying something new or reaching out to a new prospective book buyer, so always choose a specific audience for testing and record your results. That way you will qualify it as a great promotion to use as you move ahead.

TEST BY TIMING

You may run a promotion, then realize it was bad timing. A simple and smart thing to do is to try it again. If you ran the promotion during the summer and it did little, next time try doing it in the spring to reach readers gathering books for their summer reading. If you ran a weekend promotion designed to bring people to your blog for a contest and it failed, try running it again, this time during the week. The majority of your blog followers might read blogs at work during their lunchtime and be too busy over the weekends to look at blogs.

If you are running a Twitter campaign to get people to grab your free book, try running it on a Monday, a Wednesday, and a Friday. Then carefully log how much activity was recorded during each day. This can serve you very well, because now you will know which days of the week are most effective for all of your Twitter activity.

Do a specific promotion during each season to determine when responses are strongest. Try timing your activities to overlap with major events, like national lighthouse week, national gardener's week, or national coffee lovers' week.

If you're doing two different promotions at the same time, try conducting your activity for one of those promotions on the first and second week of the month, and the second promotion on the third and forth weeks of the month. Being focused will always prove more effective for your bottom line. Also, remember that your documentation is everything. Knowing exactly when you ran each promotion will help you to determine which promotion and cross market worked best and brought the most sales.

CONTROL ACTIVITY

To test by controlling your activity requires a little discipline. Even though you've stepped away from the author centipede mentality, you still have good author friends you talk to in writers groups and on-line, and there may even be a few you discuss marketing strategies with. Always remember to focus your promotions on your unique elements drawn from your SUPER Genre development. You will still be a bit of a lone wolf, because no other author has your story elements. They set you apart and identify target audiences your author friends can't approach. You can take advantage of good ideas when they come along, knowing you have a far more targeted strategy and focused audiences to speak to.

Having a group of authors you share promotional ideas, successes and strategies with can be a very good thing, but always control your promotional activities. For example, if two of your marketing author friends have decided to do a free book giveaway month to a general prospective book buyer target through their social networks, you can certainly join in, but by controlling your activity you can draw much more from this basic promotional idea. During the first week of the month, offer your free book giveaway promotion to one of your unique hook cross markets through your blog. On the second week of the month, while your friends are still blasting their free book promotion to the same audience on Twitter, you can promote your free book promotion to your unique hook cross market target audience through your social networks. On the third week of the month, you might choose to offer your free book promotion to a secondary unique hook cross market by guest blogging at blogger's site that focused on your unique hook. On the fourth week of the month, you might decide to promote your free book offer through your unique hook yahoo group cross markets.

By using the same promotional concept your author friends used – a free book giveaway month – you have reached out to a total of four different cross markets. And the best part about it is that no other author interfered with your communication to those markets. Watch your sales and determine which weeks worked best, which targets and strategies gave away more free books, and which directions failed.

CONTESTS AND GIVEAWAYS

Contests and giveaways are great ways to test markets. Choose one of your cross market targets based on your unique hooks and create a contest you will promote only to that particular target book buyer. Use your Twitter, Facebook, blog, and guest blogging efforts as well as Yahoo! Groups and even street teams to get the message out to this prospective book buyer that you are running a contest. When it's over, gauge how successful it was. It will be pure information because you haven't promoted the contest to any other general or secondary cross market. The results will be revealing, clearly telling you if the market is responsive, strong, and loyal.

TEST BY LOCATION

Testing by location is a cool idea, especially if your unique hooks connect strongly with different locations of the country or world. This is where street teams can be a great tool.

Many authors have created street teams of loyal fans to help get the word out in their local areas about the author's books. These street team members ask for the book in libraries and at bookstores. They chat up the book at book clubs and various organizations. They use their on-line and personal social networks to talk about and promote the author's books.

Street teams can be a wonderful tool for testing by location. For this example, let's say country music is the unique hook and cross market. Plan a promotion. It could be a contest, a giveaway, a chance to talk live on the phone with the author, a buy one get one free books promo, a swag giveaway or whatever you like. Choose a specific city or location like Dallas, Texas and set your Dallas street team loose. Help your team members out by letting everyone know that you're running a promotion in Dallas. Use your Twitter, Facebook, blog, and even send press releases to Dallas newspapers, magazines, library newsletters, radio, and television stations. Creating a promotion for Dallas alone where people using a code can purchase one of your books and get the second one for free is a great way to implement and follow your sales. After a month of promoting in Dallas, set your Seattle, Washington street team loose and see what happens there.

You might learn some interesting things. You might discover that you sell more books based on your country music cross market in Seattle than you do in Dallas. Could it be that you've already become known in Dallas, but are news to Seattle book buyers? Or could it be that there are more people in Seattle who fit your cross market profile than you expected? The results of testing by location might uncover the fact that one city has a dedicated street team, and another has a weaker street team. Either way, you've tested by location, discovered information to help you tap into larger prospective book buyer audiences, and sold more books.

CODE WORDS AT WORK

A good way to gauge results when running one promotion to two different cross markets at the same time is to create a code or password. You can ask your lighthouse lovers target to type in the code word BLUE when they comment on your blog. The code word will enter them into a contest to win a free book. Then ask your seaside lifestyle cross market to type in the code word RED when direct messaging you on Twitter. Keeping track of how many REDS and BLUES you receive will help you see which of the two cross markets is more effective and active.

Remember, just because one cross market might show more activity than another, doesn't mean that the lower response group is a bust. It might mean that you need more time with that specific cross market, or that the approach wasn't strong enough for that audience. Code words work best when the topic of the contest is appealing to both cross markets; otherwise you are sure to see a lopsided statistic.

You can create codes with a special note or offer that can be easily traced. For example, marketing to one specific group and asking them to comment on your Facebook page in response to an upcoming event or specific question is good. This means that you've built your awareness well and those readers are reacting exactly as you wish.

JOURNALING

As mentioned earlier, maintaining good records of everything you do will help you be more effective and efficient as you grow and move ahead. If you do a lot of speaking engagements, journal information like how many people attended, their general age, how interactive the group was, how many bought books and how many had their books signed. Another small bit of information that is valuable has to do with how long it took for you to leave the venue. If a lot of people wanted to chat and be social afterward, it tells you that you were appreciated. You might want to request another opportunity to speak with that group when your next book is released.

Journaling will also help you track which groups or organizations were helpful in bringing in their members for your event, and which were not. Reading your notes might help you identify where you wrongly chose a cross market and where you can benefit greatly by expanding a cross market.

Make other notes about things like the weather that day, the time of year and nearness to the holidays, road construction difficulties attendees might have encountered, and reasons the attendance might have been small. For example, if a local women's auxiliary group has booked you to do a reading and book signing for your romance book, there are things you need to note. Has the group ever had authors speak at their meetings before? Are they all older women who don't like to come out in snowy or rainy weather? Is it during summertime vacations? Or winter snow bird vacations? Is it near the Christmas holidays, Mother's Day, or the Fourth of July?

Often the person who runs the group will volunteer this information either before scheduling the date, or after the results are poor. Always record your contact names and information and always follow through by thanking the group for letting you speak there.

A year's worth of journaling can be a goldmine, save you time and energy and help you focus on groups, promotions, cross markets, and concepts that are worth repeating.

ELIMINATION

Yes, elimination is a wonderful testing tool. If you are extremely active on Twitter but have not been able to gauge whether Twitter is effective for your promotional efforts, simply eliminate it for a few weeks during a promotion and see what happens. Have you been consistently doing three or four promotions at the same time for months? Eliminate one and watch your numbers. If they don't drop, eliminate another one. If they do drop, replace the eliminated promotion and try eliminating a different one. This process can help you streamline your activities and allow you more time to try new ones, simply by eliminating the ones that aren't working efficiently for you.

You can eliminate a cross market and watch your numbers. You can eliminate a specific geographic location or eliminate a certain cross market blog you write every other month and see what happens. Testing by elimination can reveal a lot of things you need to know. It's in our human nature to sit on our laurels and enjoy the success, but it's important to keep in mind that even great strategies run their course and need to be either eliminated or tweaked. Staying on top of your strategies and testing them at regular intervals helps keep your efforts   effective and streamlined.

AVOID THE FUN TRAP

One final note about testing. It's very easy to simply keep a particular strategy or promotion alive just because it's fun. I'm the last person to tell you that you shouldn't have fun with your cross marketing efforts, but keep a sharp eye on the results. Knowing a promotion will not garner huge results and doing it just to have fun is one thing. But spinning your wheels in hopes of gaining great sales from that same concept is foolish. Time is money, and if you want to reach your sales goals, limit the not-so-effective promotions and focus on the ones that make big sales.

CONTROLLING COSTS

The Difference between Free and Cheap – I've never known a writer who wasn't starving for something. Some want more time, some need ideas, most desire a champion to fight for them, and in this time of shifting publishing industry paradigm, all of them need to market and promote. The problem is that most authors just don't have the money. Enter the internet, and every crazy free or no charge scam imaginable. It's just the tip of the iceberg and very little of it is designed for long term results. Many are designed to feed our egos, and most take advantage of a writer's ignorance about the publicity, marketing, or promotions process. Always remember, you get what you pay for.

At this point, I'd like to explore a few specific words authors on a tight budget seem to hone in on. Free, cheap, inexpensive, reasonable, and value or value added.

Free – This is easily the most powerful word in the English language, maybe even more effective than the word "Fire!" Free falls into the category with words like easy, stress free, and child's play. Come on now, you're a writer. Has anything in this process been easy, stress free, or child's play? What makes you think promoting your book will go any more smoothly than writing it? Free is where the phrase bait and switch comes in to play. Let's take an example: Press release services.

You've just written a sterling press release announcing the release of your book, or where you'll be doing a book signing event, or when you'll   be interviewed on a radio show. Now you need to create a list for where to send it. But it's more complicated than that, you must specify who will receive it at each target media location. There are options here. You could painstakingly create a killer media press release list of your own by doing research and compiling everything specific to your needs. That may be free, but it sure isn't easy. Or you can seek out an already developed list, so you troll the web and low and behold, you find not one but several press release list services that boast the word free. You're in like Flint, right? Wrong. Take a closer look.

Yes, for free you will have your press release go out, but you won't know to whom, nor can you specify an industry or subject in which the release should be categorized. You need to wait two full days for the company to screen your press release and deem it inoffensive before you beautiful press release is actually sent out. Seems reasonable. In fact, even paid press release email services take the time to look over your submission. Here's the catch. For free, you don't get to add any attachments, you don't know where the release is going, you don't know if it was ever received, so you have no idea how or with whom you should follow up. On top of all that, you won't even receive proof it went out.

I'm not condemning free press release email services. I'm only pointing out that such services make it extremely difficult to gauge the success of your press releases.

If you go back to the main page of that press release mailing service page, you will see a chart. The chart that shows you what you get if you pay for it. On-line email press release services range from free to hundreds of dollars per release. The super expensive services are not a scam. They include AP wire service, international targets, and client specifics down to the smallest detail. Those are the services that provide reports that gauge success.

Nothing is free, at least nothing that works. Sorry.

Cheap – Okay, time to look at cheap. You need to self promote, there are no two ways about it. Without tooting your own horn, you will be lost in the tall weeds. Cheap directions can include a few free things, but in this category, everything requires your careful, watchful eye and diligence. Website creation can be created cheaply, but the website doesn't need to look cheap, so it may be beneficial to get some help in that area. If money is too tight, think about trading services instead of paying cash. For example, a friend who builds beautiful websites may occasionally need a writer to pen the blurbs for his/her clients.

Blogging is cheap. Well, in most cases it's free, but your time isn't, so budget your time carefully to assure that your blog is updated and promoted regularly. The same goes for Twitter, Facebook, and all the other social networks. Saying you're on Twitter and actually tweeting regularly are two different things. I have to laugh when clients tell me Twitter does nothing for them. A little exploration explains how they've done nothing to make Twitter a viable tool. Things like having a website, a blog, and social networks are the life blood of making yourself and your book known. Technically social networks and blogs are free, but it's a strategic investment of time and energy that make this cheap direction valuable.

Inexpensive – It's a relative concept and depends on how empty your pockets really are. The best way to seek and utilize the illusive inexpensive strategies is to create them. Think outside the box. Maybe you can't get on *Good Morning America*, but why aren't you trying to get on your local public television shows? Maybe speaking at the biggest bookstore chain isn't possible due to scheduling, but look around. Aren't there fifteen small independent book stores and libraries nearby? Maybe you can't purchase a quarter-page ad in the city newspaper, but printing out flyers and posting them at your local market, beauty salon, your pet's vet, your dentist's office or any business related to your book subject just may be extremely effective.

The difference between expensive and inexpensive is elbow grease. Trust me, you can work around anything and get astounding results if you just think creatively and work it to the bone. Lots of small efforts lead to big exposure that just may put you on the map sooner than you think.

Reasonable – What's reasonable for you? It depends on your goals. If you've self-published and have put no efforts in creating your platforms, marketing, or publicity, it's highly unlikely you'll be on the *New York Times Best Sellers List* by Christmas. Finding reasonable solutions to building success often takes an author back to the original question. Why did they want to write a book in the first place? Make a pot of coffee, grab a note pad, refresh your mind about the answer to that question, and start getting reasonable.

Writing is a career, not a pastime, not a fun thing we like to do. It's a business. If you opened a corner coffee shop, you'd be taking on an inventory based business with built-in competition. You'd do whatever you had to do to bring people off the sidewalk and through your doors. You'd create specials and promotions. Know why you'd work this hard? You'd do it because your failure would be painfully obvious when the "Out of Business" sign went up in the window. When you're on your own, it's tougher.

Now, let's imagine that instead of being independent, you buy a Starbuck's franchise. Now you have guidelines, training, specific products, national advertising, and an already established following. Cool huh? But guess what,?

You still have to be there to open the doors, hire the employees, stock the shelves, make acceptable vanilla lattes, and meet expectations. You have a lot of support but failure is still a looming possibility.

Everyone has to work at it, and in the case of authors, reasonable is all about knowing your limitations and needs. It's about understanding the professionals you need, choosing them carefully, and working with them to get the success you want. Whether you opened a tiny corner coffee shop or a shiny new Starbucks, you still have the same goals.

Good professionals know how to help you reach them. Don't randomly hire marketing experts, publicists, advertising agencies, or even personal assistants. Make sure the relationship is reasonable for you, your wallet, and your target goals.

Oh, and just like owning that coffee shop, with hiring comes possible dismissal. Know how to say, "enough" and move on.

Value or value added –Promotions are about glitz and glamour, loud bongs and flashy lights, and gaining fans and sales results.

The problem is, as the creator of the product, we tend to get mesmerized by all that sparkle. Like a dog that suddenly stops mid-stride because he notices a squirrel, we have a habit of falling head over heels in love with the ego-feeding super promotions. This doesn't mean those particular promotions are bad or ineffective or even ill advised. They may be perfect for your book, but the author's responsibility is to stop drooling, take a deeper look, and decide intelligently. Explore the value of the promotion and seek out the added value because therein lies the power.

For example, who doesn't get excited about things like book videos, high profile ads, audio books created by famous actors, a possible movie deal, or international interest for translated publication of their book? It's so heart-pounding, it makes the head spin. There are three things you must think about before you swoon with expectant riches.

- Cool as it may be, does the promotion really serve to reach your reader target? Many promos blast off about reaching a million viewers, but honestly, if you've written a dark literary novel about the history of the Druids, and a large portion of the viewers boasted happen to be YA readers who prefer sparkly vampires, this may not be the promotion for you. How will you know if you don't demand proof of the demographic receiving the promo info? And yes, you certainly can demand proof, after all, you are paying for it.

- Is it necessary? It makes perfect sense to do an audio book version of your amazing Druid book, but is it really necessary to hire Russell Crowe to do the recorded read? Isn't it the story that's important? Wouldn't an unknown with the perfect resonant voice do just as well and cost much less than your mortgage and/or first born male child?
- Where's the added value? Some of these services have taken things several steps further to help assure success for not only their product, but their client's promotion. For example, never, ever even consider having a book video produced unless the company offers a strong marketing package to make it all work. Yes, it'll cost a bit more, but what good is having a cool book video that no one sees? Ask for the added value packages, look them over carefully and choose the one most likely to create the success you want.
- Watch your budget, watch your choices and always look for value when you pay for promotional services.

MAGICIAN'S TRIAL ASSIGNMENT

There are rules for everything and nothing worthwhile comes easy. The cool thing about planning your own strategy for success through cross marketing efforts is that you get to determine the rules you will follow and the efforts you're willing to put forth. You are the magician here. Some magicians are fantastic, some, not so much. To decide what kind of sale making magician you want to be, you need to set a few standards for yourself.

Start with your goals. It's important that you not limit yourself with this. This is not about being realistic to the point of avoiding disappointment; this is all about setting your bar high and reaching for it.

For this assignment, set your sales goals by number of books and not dollar amounts. Here's an example of a basic goal plan:

- **0 – 90 days**   **1,000 books**
- **90 days to 6 months**   **5,000 books**
- **Year 1**   **10,000 books**
- **Year 2**   **25,000 books**

Your next magic trick must determine how you plan to reach those goals.

- **0 – 90 days**   **1,000 books**
  - Regular book marketing strategies
  - Cross marketing target #1
  - Cross marketing target #2

- **90 days to 6 months**   **5,000 books**
  - Add cross marketing venue #1
  - Add cross marketing venue #2
  - Add cross marketing target #3

- **Year 1**   **10,000 books**
  - Using all cross marketing targets and venues
  - Run promotion #1
  - Run promotion #2
  - Run promotion #3
  - Develop publicity support strategy

- **Year 2**   **25,000 books**
  - Release book #2
  - Use all cross marketing targets
  - Use all cross market venues
  - Promotional launch event
  - Run all promotions
  - Implement publicity event to support charity

Naturally you will need to create all the cross market targets, venues, relationships, and promotions, and write your second book. But without a plan, little will happen in the way of meeting your book sales goals.

Building a strategy with vague steps like this is a perfect way to help you as you grow. For example, the targets and venues for your first six months of marketing might shift and change for your first year, and again for your second year. You might release new books quicker or slower than you think you might. You might stumble onto a new cross market you never imagined and implement it into your plan. Above it all and right in front of you are your goals, bold and proud and waiting for you to reach them with all the tools you have at your disposal.

Remember to test your results often, eliminate efforts that don't work, constantly seek ways to reach your unique hook targets and cross markets, and avoid the author centipede mentality.

Scry Me a River of Money!

Wouldn't it be fantastic to have a crystal ball to tell us how successful our cross marketing efforts will be? Since neither you nor I have one of those, the best advice I can give is to be determined, tenacious, and consistent and you will be successful! In the meantime, I thought you might like to know a little history about the crystal ball.

According to *Paranormal Investigation of NYC*, the history of the crystal ball can be traced back as far as the medieval period in central Europe (between 500 – 1500 AD) and in Scandinavia (1050 – 1500 AD).

There have always been fortune-tellers throughout history as well. Religious sciences tell us, for example, about Apollo's (the Greek God of prophesy) oracle priestess, Pythia who had powers (1500 B.C.). Used by seers, fortune-tellers, psychics, and sorcerers, the crystal ball seems to be one of the most well-known and popular forms of scrying, as well as a divination tool. Scrying is the name given to the ancient technique of gazing into an object such as a crystal ball or a bowl of water. It is usually physically, ritually, or spiritually, cleansed before each use for purification purposes.

When a crystal is used, scrying is known as crystallomancy. Using crystals in the divination of one's past, present, and future traditionally played a key role in the decision-making process of many powerful leaders throughout history. One of the most notable was King Arthur, who sought out the advice and prophecies of Merlin the Magician. In more recent history, Nancy Reagan, the first lady of then President Ronald Reagan, avidly used psychics to help plan her husband's domestic and foreign affairs. One of the earliest uses of crystals in scrying comes from the Druids who used Beryllium Aluminum Silicate (Beryl), a natural gemstone whose characteristics range from transparent to translucent. Scottish Highlanders termed these objects "stones of power".

Early crystal balls were made from Beryl. Later the Beryl was replaced by spheres made of rock crystal. The reason crystals in particular became important tools for scrying and other metaphysical aspects is because of their inherent characteristics of transparency and regularity of their patterns, called symmetry. Additionally, the energetic fields of crystals influence what the scryer "sees" on a very subtle and often esoteric level.

PART 7
TIME MANAGEMENT SKILLS

"If you don't know where you're going, you'll end up someplace else.."

~ Yogi Berra

One way to protect against failure is to plan. Another powerful way to protect against failure is to manage your time well. There are several reasons why authors must manage their time. Some work full time jobs then write and market their books in the evenings and on weekends. Some authors are raising children, or caring for ill family members or elderly parents. Some authors are lucky enough to work from home and have the peace and quiet of the whole day – in between the paying job responsibilities – to write and market. Still others are retired or financially blessed enough to simply write for a living. Of course those authors are plagued by everyone they know, assuming that they're home all day and have nothing else to do, so they might as well run a few errands or do a few favors with all their free time.

No author has it easy, and without efficient and effective time management, nothing will get done. Here are a few tips to help you do everything you need and still live a sane, productive, and fairly normal life. In the next section, we will explore the best way to create simple, easy to use worksheets for each responsibility.

SOCIAL MEDIA TIME MANAGEMENT

Yes, you must use Twitter and Facebook, and you must blog and maintain your author and book websites. You must update your media rooms and events calendars on those websites too. And this only represents the basic marketing strategies. For advanced strategies like niche and cross marketing, you also need to expand your platforms and develop broader audiences based on the unique hook elements inside your book.

The trick to all of this is to be strategic with the time you spend on each element of this list. Spend no more than one hour each weekday on your social media. Spend no more than one additional hour over the course of a week to expand your friends and follower list to accommodate your unique hook targets and cross market audience.

Marketing is creating awareness for you and your book and your social networks are a major part of your marketing. One can't happen without the other, so be tight and efficient with your social media time. It's not social playtime; it's a powerful business tool. Use it well and never let it steal away your valuable time.

PRESERVING YOUR WRITING TIME

What time of the day are you most productive? Every day I ask an author survey question on my Facebook page and when I ask this one, I'm always amazed at the varied and amazing solutions authors come up with. Authors are a resilient bunch and when bitten by the need to write, there is no limit to how they will find the time to be successful. Are you an early morning writer? Do you love to write when the house is dark and quiet late at night? Are you a sneak-it-in-here-and-there kind of writer? The kind who manages to record bits of dialogue or plot ideas while sitting in traffic, or email yourself ideas during your lunch hour? Are you the kind of author who needs a block of time to be productive, or are you the kind who can write in the midst of confusion and distractions? Do you write only on Sundays from sun up until midnight, or is Sunday the only day you don't write? I've heard a hundred different ways in which writers scratch out writing time. I wrote my first book while I was a professional chef. I'd work in a hot kitchen from ten in the morning until ten at night then go home, make a pot of coffee, and write until four the next morning. Then I'd sleep and wake up and do it all over again.

Writers write. We can't help it. In addition to writing, authors must market, because if our books don't sell, there's little point in writing another one. This is the reason our marketing time must be tightly managed, so that we can protect our writing time. One hand washes the other, so never imagine it's okay to sacrifice one for the other. At times it'll feel like a vicious cycle, but trust me, every effort is building upon the other and if you're not spinning your wheels on unproductive activity, you will see your success.

Protect your writing time like a mama bear. Let nothing interrupt or steal it away, and give it all you have. Don't imagine that you need to sit at the computer screen and play solitaire for a few minutes before you can hunker down and write. I'm certainly guilty of that. Recognizing how important those precious hours for writing are is the key to never letting it slip through your fingers. Wrap your arms around it and protect it like your favorite child. The muse is fickle and if we ignore her one time too many, she will move on to another author hoping for inspiration.

Writing is a performance art. It requires the mind, the creativity, the keyboard, and the promise of completion. Never sacrifice a moment of your writing time. It's a gift.

MAKING TIME FOR EDUCATION

Is there nothing left to learn? Of course not. Even the top ten bestselling authors can learn something about their craft or marketing or even ways to develop creative solutions. We need to remember to make time for educating ourselves to be better writers.

This could mean taking an occasional day trip to the zoo or the river or even the city. Walking in various environments sharpens our observation skills and polishes our imagination. In *The Artist's Way*, author Julia Cameron calls these little day trips the artist date. She encourages readers to take their inner artist out on a play date to see something of the world. In return the inner artist will reward them with creativity and expansion. An artist date can be a trip around the world or a trip across town. It's an educational tool you need to give yourself every once in a while.

Other tools include seeking out other artistic endeavors. I recall going to a symphony series in Los Angeles a few years ago. It was called *What Makes it Great?* In this series, a quartet or trio or an entire symphony orchestra, under the guidance of the instructor, explored the various note and timing within classical pieces of music that made it great. During each of the four part series, I clearly recall listening to the music and connecting it to what makes writing great. It inspired me to delve deeper into my own craft to uncover how and why it works and how to improve it.

On any given day there are hundreds of on-line workshops priced from a mere fifteen dollars per student to hundreds of dollars, all covering the craft of writing, the skill of writing screen plays, the techniques of plot and character development, and the magic of creating a great book video. There are university classes galore, available in classrooms and on-line. There are event panels of authors, publishing editors, literary agents, and even marketing experts all prepared to pass their knowledge and expertise on to you.

Educate yourself in everything from craft to editing perfection to advanced marketing strategies. Fit these educational opportunities into your time management schedule. Grow and your success will grow with you.

FINDING TIME TO RECHARGE

What do you do to rejuvenate and replenish your creative self? If the answer is nothing more than the booming sound of confused silence, it's time to rethink your life. Writing is more than a job, it's a passion and a commitment that builds and grows on inspiration. If all an author does is pound out word counts and pay attention to sales numbers, all the fun is drained right out of it.

Mark off time on your monthly calendar for fun. Yes, fun. – the laughing with your friends, having a drink, and going to a movie kind of fun. Fun that requires riding a bike or climbing a mountain. Learn how to cook Italian food, or speak Chinese. Do something that gives you joy and revitalizes you. Go to an amusement park. Take skiing lessons. Learn how to arrange flowers or perform Tai Chi. Belly dance. Play softball. In other words, do something really fun and put it on your schedule in ink. You need this. We all need it.

ROLE MODELS AND MENTORS. DOES ANYONE KNOW HOW TO GET THERE?

At this point I felt it was important to briefly touch on the subject of getting to the success you're hoping for. Seeking role models in the publishing industry, especially among authors, can be daunting. You might fall in love with a top ten bestselling author writing in our genre, but short of stalking, how can you really determine how their success was created? Make no mistake, success is created, especially for writers.

Setting aside the basic requirements of writing very well, plotting with exceptional skill, and developing characters a reader can't forget, there are   other vital things an author needs to do to create success. Leadership can be found in your social and professional networks, but be a savvy customer and even if you're only taking free advice, confirm that your contact is legitimate. Leadership can be hiding in your writing groups and critique groups or among the authors you know, but which one should you listen to? Who has had the best sales and most effective marketing or promotions? Who hasn't? And therein lies the rub.

It's time to pick up the mirror and take a good hard look at yourself. Take inventory of your activities, time management, and goals, and determine what success means to you. There's a way to find the correct role models to help you, but in the end, you'll discover that only you can lead your career.

- **Be Prepared** – Look at the most successful authors out there. Explore their websites and follow them on Twitter and Facebook. How active are they? How interactive? It's no fluke that authors like Neil Gaiman are active and interactive on Twitter. He knows that being visible is part of marketing and creating awareness for himself, no matter what he writes or when his new book is released. He's connected to his fans, and you should be too. Have an active website with a strong media room that invites the press to take a look at you. Put creative elements into your book website to attract readers. Build an effective social network following of readers and prospective book buyers for your book and genre. That way, when you have something to tweet about, you'll be talking to the right people. Build a committed blog following of readers and prospective book buyers by focusing your posts on the subjects within your book that attract them. It's what the most successful authors do. The difference is that you are doing it based on the unique hooks in your book and efficiently using advanced cross marketing techniques.
- **Skip no Steps** – Now that you're prepared to lead yourself to success, be careful to follow all the steps and rules for marketing, promotions, and publicity. Marketing is creating awareness. Without it, promotions are less likely to work and your publicity might sound like crickets after midnight. The rules are simple. First, market well by creating the right following and holding their attention. Next, promote with power, by creating unique promotions every other author in the world *isn't* doing. And finally, use publicity wisely, by finding ways to connect with appropriate charities or charitable events that might catch the media's attention.

- **Use Creative Approaches** – You're a creative person. You wrote a great book and now you need to be creative in getting the word out. Focus on role models that have created success without following the crowd. Avoid the author centipede mentality. It's more important to stand apart than to stand with the crowd and try to shout louder. Create different ways to reach your audience. If you write romance, look for women in places other than the romance lovers' book clubs or groups. Look for them where women live – in gardening clubs, health clubs, ladies auxiliary clubs, and cooking groups. Look for them on-line and in your neighborhood. How cool would it be to do a reading, book sale, and signing at a nurse's group monthly meeting? Be different and success will come faster.

- **Watch the Arena** – Keep an eye on the industry, other authors' promotional strategies, and reader/genre trends at all times. Do this by using Twitter and Facebook to follow the news in publishing, your book's genre, book store closings, etc. Know what's going on around you, that way you can act rather than react when a change ripples through the industry.

- **Execute Strong** – Never waver. Trust in your plan and follow through. Just because other authors haven't tried it does not mean it won't work. If you've done your homework, are talking to the right target book buyer and are consistent with your efforts, it can't fail.

- **Test Results** – Always be objective. Look to your role models and see what they do. If a promotion gets quiet, it never comes back, right? That means the author has tested the results and discarded the idea for a better one. No matter how much you love a promotional idea, it could fall short and you will need to move on to the next idea.

We all love following a leader and are all looking for role models. We want to know everything they do. How do they come up with their story ideas? How do they create awareness? How do they promote? How do they manage their time? They can lead us to some interesting revelations about the process of selling books and creating a buzz, but their book is not your book. So, next time you wonder which way to go to find success, look in the mirror. Be the leader you can be for your own career.

KEEPING YOUR MARKETING MOMENTUM

How do you keep the marketing love alive? We authors have a massive load on our shoulders. We have to work to pay the bills, take care of family, socialize occasionally with friends, write books, and promote and market them too. It's a lot to ask of anyone, but asking an author who is basically a creative thinker to suddenly become an analytical, business like person is sort of like asking a dog to be a cat two days a week.

I'm sure you've all faced the dilemma of starting a marketing strategy for your book and discovering that after some time, that fantastic strategy has sort of fizzled out. What's an author to do? We don't want to start from scratch but we can't just stop marketing and promoting or demand for our next book will be next to nothing. It's not a disaster; it's just time to put on our thinking caps again.

Creativity is creativity and if you look at marketing and promoting your books as part of the whole creative process, you are sure to find the perfect formula for success that works for you and your book.

The reason most tried and true marketing and promotional strategies fizzle out so quickly is that they are basically overused. The person hearing the message has heard it a thousand times. The key to keeping your marketing push alive is to keep it moving like a good boxer with great footwork. Here are three tips to reboot your marketing efforts that won't take a ton of time or energy, just a little creativity.

Find a New Route – It's the ugly truth. Your book is in the same genre and tapping into the same market as a thousand other books. You do what the most successful authors are doing, at least you try, but it always falls flat quickly.

This is a simple study in looking the other way, or in this case, ANOTHER way. I've always found that if everyone is taking a particular freeway at a particular time of day, it's easiest on my gas tank and my nerves to simply take a different freeway. Apply that to your marketing and everything gets a whole new light.

For example, if all the authors are slamming away on the newest trick of the day, giveaways or contests or scavenger hunts, you need to consider doing something they are not doing. In fact, this works best if it's something they never even thought about doing.

Consider creating a high visibility promotion that includes publicity. You could create a walk for cancer for zombie book lovers (in costume of course), or a blood drive where vampire authors and fans donate blood and attempt to reach a goal of a certain number of donors in a limited time. This kind of publicity gets noticed and if you are the author who created it, it has long term positive ramifications as you move ahead in your marketing.

Have you thought about doing an event at a singles group or meeting of the local yoga club? Trust me, singles and yoga lovers aren't all these groups talk about or all they do. These people like to read too. If you offer to do a reading and Q&A at a meeting of the local policewomen or dental assistants, they might jump for joy. Have you considered doing a reading and book signing for a retirement community? They are desperate for entertaining and fun opportunities for their residents. These organizations are always open to interesting speakers for their meetings and gatherings. And while every other author in your genre is pounding away, trying to give away a free book on Twitter, you're signing a selling twenty or thirty books at the ladies auxiliary meeting right in your home town.

Looking elsewhere is always a great way to keep your sales active and growing. When you go back to the regular grind of Twitter and Facebook, you suddenly have some really fun and interesting experiences to talk about.

Change the Odds – Ever been to Vegas? Even if you haven't, you know the odds and what they mean. If Dan Brown writes a book, everyone buys it. He has all the odds in his favor, a big publisher, high visibility thanks to his wonderful marketing and publicity experts, and fans by the boat loads. How are we supposed to stand against all that?

Simple. Change the odds. For example, even if your book touches on similar subjects, has a similar story and similar characters, something about your book is different and extremely unique. The only way to battle something as formidable as the top ten bestsellers, is to find your hooks and make sure they're sharp.

Is your hook the unique character traits in your book that you haven't used yet? If your main character is a cigar expert, you need to tap into the cigar industry. If he's into fine whiskey, there's another audiences. Cross marketing is the magic of changing the odds. If you can cross market your book to music teachers or the home building industry because your story and primary characters connected with that subject, you are tapping into new markets.

Here's the kicker, you're doing this without an expensive publicist or big publisher; you're doing this as you. This really does change the odds because now you can sit at the same poker table with any top ten bestselling author in the world.

Look Outside – When you want to do some marketing, where do you look? In most cases you look to other authors. Yes, other authors are doing what authors do and I'm not telling you to stop doing the tried and true marketing techniques. Keep marketing to your genre groups, continue to seek book reviews, and reach out to book clubs. It's how the inside track runs. Isn't it time to blaze new trails?

I'm suggesting that you look outside the publishing world for interesting and powerful ideas.

Did you notice a slogan on the passing exterminator's van that caught your fancy? A billboard that used just the right visual and verbal impact for the product? A radio or television campaign that you can't forget? Marketing and promotion is going on all around us and there are some fantastic approaches just outside the publishing world. Lift your head and look around.

If you take a week and keep a small note pad at your side, you will find yourself observing and jotting down cool ideas from all kinds of products and services. These concepts impressed and intrigued you. They sparked your imagination and made you smile. All you have to do is think them through and consider whether one of those approaches will work for your book. Maybe you can't do a teaser promotion on the radio like you heard for the new laundry detergent with bleach, but you can do something similar with teasers in your blogs, on Twitter, or on Facebook. If the fun event to raise money and awareness for the local zoo can't exactly work for your book, perhaps there's an element of that event that you can implement for your own marketing.

All I'm suggesting is that you can seriously impact your marketing approach if you just step away from the computer screen and look outside. Marketing is happening all around. Take a change of scenery and allow yourself to be influenced by some of the best of our time.

So, there you go. Three tips for keeping your book marketing momentum alive and vibrant. There's no reason to sit and tap your toe, waiting for a new idea to occur to you. Look around. Change your thinking. Change your odds. Be creative.

Timing is Everything

The House of Parliament's iconic clock tower is one of London's most famous landmarks. According to the official London Visitor Guide at http://www.visitlondon.com/, Big Ben is the name given to the massive bell inside the clock tower, which weighs more than 13,760 kg (13 tons). Here are a few cool Big Ben facts:

- Each dial is seven meters in diameter
- The minute hands are 4.2 meters long and weigh about 100 kg (including counterweights)
- The numbers are approximately 60 cm long
- There are 312 pieces of glass in each clock dial

- A special light above the clock faces is illuminated when parliament is in session
- Big Ben's timekeeping is strictly regulated by a stack of coins placed on the huge pendulum
- Big Ben has rarely stopped. Even after a bomb destroyed the Commons chamber during the Second World War, the clock tower survived and Big Ben continued to strike the hours
- The chimes of Big Ben were first broadcast by the BBC on December, 31, 1923, a tradition that continues to this day
- In June 2012 the House of Commons announced that the clock tower was to be renamed the Elizabeth Tower in honor of Queen Elizabeth II's Diamond Jubilee

SMOKE AND MIRRORS ASSIGNMENT

For this assignment, I thought I'd ask you to view it from a completely different creative angle. Let's imagine you are an opera singer. You're in demand all over the world. You have a loving family and children, and elderly parents who are dealing with failing health. You have bills to pay and chores to do. In other words, you could be an accountant, except that instead of adding and subtracting numbers, you are singing your heart out every single day.

Put yourself deeply into this person's life and create a time management plan for them. There is a lot going on in their life, and if they drop even one ball, demand for their skill and talent could disappear. Schedule what time they will wake and when they will go to bed. When they will practice and when they will perform. Think about when they will seek out new opportunities and when they will participate in the charities of their choice. When will they spend time with their family and when will they explore creative options for growth. When will they make improvements on their craft, and when will they simply have some fun. Create a calendar for this opera singer, then simply change their name to yours.

PART 8
CROSS MARKETING MAGIC WORKSHEET STRATEGIES

"Only those who will risk going too far can possibly find out how far one can go."

~ T.S. Eliot

The magic is in the planning, the practicing, and the perfecting! I absolutely love having worksheets. They help me manage my time and record important information. When I was a child, I loved having to-do lists, especially when I could cross off each item on the list with pride. Maybe I'm a little anal, or maybe I'm just a little nuts, but these things really work for me.

In this section, I will either show you a possible worksheet covering the various responsibilities, or explain how to create one.

SOCIAL MEDIA TIME MANAGEMENT WORKSHEET

Social Networking Daily Checklist

TWITTER

Image acceptable?	*Yes*
9:10 AM – 9:20 AM	*Done, logged off at 9:20 AM*
Social tweets	*4*
Promo tweets	*4*
Retweets	*3*
Followers growth	*Followed 3 from urban fantasy book clubs*
4:40 PM – 4:50 PM	*Done, logged off at 4:51*
Social tweets	*6*
Promo tweets	*2*

Retweets	*4*
Followers growth	*Followed 4 from last week's #FF (Follow Friday)*
Total time spent	*21 minutes*

FACEBOOK

Image acceptable?	*Yes*
Initial post of the day	*Done*
Social Facebook	*Asked one question of the day and responded to 2 posts in the News Feed*
Promo posts	*1 promoting new blog entry, posted same at 8 Facebook groups*
Friends growth	*Accepted 2 new friends and requested friendship of 2 new urban fantasy book clubs*
Initial post response	*Comments and "liked" comments posted on original post*
Total time spent	*15 minutes*

EMAIL LISTS

Added to fan list	*4, as requested through book website and blogs*
Added to media contacts	*6 - 4 local media contacts and 2 updated contacts*
Added to general list	*6, new friends met at ballgame, interested in book news*
Total time spent	*10 minutes*

GROUP MEMBERSHIPS

Search new	*Joined 2 Facebook urban fantasy lovers groups and joined 1 new fiction readers fan group on Linked-In*
Responses to existing	*Looked through daily digest emails from my LinkedIn and Yahoo! Groups, chose to exit from 2 and responded to 1*
Total time spent	*10 minutes*

FACE TO FACE NETWORKING

| #1 | *Talked about book at the dentist's during checkup, posted flyer for the book in employee lounge* |
| #2 | *Chatted about book while helping at son's school lunch* |

#3	*Talked about book with waitress who mentioned she loves vampires*
Total Time Spent	*5 extra minutes beyond normal time spent at dentist, school or restaurant.*

ADDING CROSS MARKET TARGET AUDIENCES TO ALL SOCIAL NETWORKS

Total time spent	*Twitter, Facebook, blogging, and joining new cross marketing groups, all done on weekday afternoons, 10 minutes each day*

Total time spent on all social networking,
   Monday through Friday   61 minutes

Total time spent expanding target audiences   50 minutes

SUPER GENRE GAME WORKSHEET

For this one, I'm just going to give you a little direction. A few critical steps will help you create amazing expanded and SUPER Genres for your book.

- **Step One – Reread your book.** Simple, right? So many authors write wonderful books, plow into their marketing and promotions along with all the other authors in the author centipede, and along the way, simply forget the wonderful unique hooks they had written in the story in the first place. It might seem crazy, but sit down and read your book again. It will help you to locate and identify the magic in it, and spur wonderful marketing directions as you read.
- **Step Two – Create your expanded genres.** If your book is a romance, expand it. First play the genre game and add the various subgenres that might apply. Then think about three major unique hooks in your story that will spur a ton of ideas. For example:
  - Romance/ historical/ seaside lifestyle
  - Romance/ historical/ vintage clothing
  - Romance/ historical/ lighthouse restoration

In this case you've successfully created three cross marketing directions by expanding your genre. Within that list should be at least one that connects with a possible charity.

- **Step Three – Create your SUPER GENRES.** Time to get crazy, have some fun and stretch it out as far as you can. Under each of your three expanded genres, you will now create SUPER Genres of as many as twenty genre descriptions. For example:
  - Romance/ historical/ seaside lifestyle/ horse and buggy/ Victorian seaside hotels/ seaside small town life/ etc./ etc./ etc.

Once you've created your SUPER Genres, you will have several very promising directions to go for your cross marketing efforts. But without rereading your book first, you might have forgotten a few of them completely.

NICHE AND CROSS MARKET WORKSHEET

Every element of your cross marketing strategy should be documented and tested. It's not good enough to try something and discover a few weeks later that it really worked but you're not sure why or how. To build momentum for your book's visibility, interest, and sales you need to know what you're attempting, what your goals are, and you must clearly document how successful or unsuccessful each effort is.

You will be running at least two different cross marketing approaches at the same time, plus your standard marketing to the obvious target markets, but how can you break it down to see which effort was successful and if you actually did everything you could to make it work? How much success makes a cross market direction worthy of additional work?

Before you create a worksheet for these efforts, here are a few critical red flags to watch out for, and among them are the biggest three that torment most authors.

- **Hope** – Oh, we so hope people will like our book that we sometimes display our baby and just wish for great results. We're looking for emotional, professional, personal, and maybe even spiritual validation. A reason to go on! Okay, maybe that's a little dramatic but you get my point. I call hope a non-strategy. It falls under the category of inaction and must always be checked at the door when testing your marketing and cross marketing, because there's easily twice as much of a   chance for criticism in an unsuspecting, ill approached cross market as there will be in the normal genre market strategy. Don't hope. Plan.

- **Imagined Credibility** – This one doesn't only apply to cross marketing, it applies to writing your book in the first place. Words you might say to yourself under the influence of imagined credibility are: *Oh, people will love this idea! People need to read more books like this.* (And my favorite*) If I just explain my reasoning they'll buy my book by the millions!* Trust me, if you have to explain anything to anyone, it's not working. That goes for your plot and your cross marketing strategy. Simplicity is what attracts people, and reality is what attracts cross markets. If you think gardening clubs will love your book because your main character has a back yard garden, you may be way off base. Be realistic with your cross marketing. It will take a lot of focus on that main character's garden to attract the attention of gardening clubs. That garden must almost *be a main character* itself. If it isn't, this would be like approaching dentist groups because one of your main character brushes his teeth once in the book. Imagined credibility is another non-strategy.

- **Fear** –Ouch, this one can put a real kibosh on your plans, no matter how well thought out and strategically successful your cross marketing ideas are. Try to look on the bright side. What are you really afraid of? If a cross market does not respond to your efforts, there's nothing lost. Face your fears, take a leap and see what happens. Fear is non-strategy #3.

All three of these cases – hope, imagined credibility, and fear – must be recognized for what they are: non-strategies and ineffective wastes of time. I usually simply mark them "DUH" because, of course, I knew better when I implemented them in the first place. So will you.

So, how do you keep track of all this cross market activity? You must create a worksheet that does the following things well:

- Develops creative exploration for cross markets
- Establishes a testing system to determine if the cross market is viable
- Expands on good ideas while eliminating the bad ideas.

You must set standards. Creating a worksheet to help you navigate through the process can be simple or a complex. It can be created on Excel spreadsheets or on a yellow lined pad. There are three primary tasks listed above and three non-strategy situations to avoid.

Because cross marketing your book is such a personal thing, I strongly encourage you to create your own worksheet, but to help you visualize, I've put together a sample cross marketing worksheet.

Remember, every book and every author is different, so make sure your worksheet is specific to your book, your genre, your subgenres, your SUPER Genres, and your sensibilities. Make the plan aggressive enough but not too complex to manage effectively. Activity and consistency are the keys to success. You must put in the work.

CROSS MARKET WORKSHEET

Book Title	*Callie's Spirit*
25 Word Synopsis	*Callie Cohen, small town seamstress, has an extraordinary client from 150 years in the past who teaches her some powerful life and love lessons*
Primary Genre	*Women's fiction*
Primary Target	*Women, 18 -60*
Possible Subgenres	*Paranormal, paranormal (light) romance, YA*

OBVIOUS MARKETS

Target 1	*Women's fiction book clubs*
Target 2	*Fans of paranormal romance and YA*
Target 3	*All my author friends (DUH, non-strategy – authors are not effective sales target)*

SUPER GENRE CROSS MARKETS

Hidden target 1	*Callie is a seamstress, possibly fashion fans would like book*
Hidden target 2	*The story takes place in the Outer Banks of S.C., possible local and tourist fans. Callie also spends a lot of time at lighthouses (there are several in the Outer Banks)*
Hidden target 3	*Historical story line might interest history buffs, historical followers of the area, and/or historical book clubs*
Hidden target 4	*Supporters of the historic lighthouses in the Outer Banks might be interested*
Hidden target 5	*Fashion design students (DUH, non-strategy – design students are more interested in learning to design than reading my book)*

Hidden target 6   *Sewing store customers*

NOTE – Use expanded genre and SUPER Genre elements to uncover more hidden targets.

PLATFORM STRATEGIES

Book website   *Must be kept active to hold primary market interest and maintain newly acquired fans from cross markets. Have regular updates on characters, area points of interest, even harsh weather reports in that area, or correlating historical events that relate to the book.*

Blog   *Write weekly blog covering the strongest theme of my book. Talk about history and the area, and work as a seamstress 150 years ago and in contemporary times. Become the expert in these areas. Guest blog at clothing, vintage clothing, and seamstress blogs.*

Social media   *Twitter, Facebook. Expand target friends and followers of the genre, sub-genre, SUPER Genres, and those interested in the book's unique hooks and cross market themes.*

Group affiliations   *Join cross market groups like lighthouse lovers groups, paranormal/ghost lovers groups, historical clothing groups. List them and remember to really join, not just show up and pitch my book. Share my book's topics and gain insight from other group members.*

Live connections   *Create connections with LIVE businesses and groups that have common interests in the unique hooks in my book like historical clubs or sewing clubs or even seaside businesses. Would the local gift store like to carry my book? Would the local library be willing to shelf my book or permit me time to speak about my book? Would the local crafts and sewing store like to display my book? All good connections. List them and schedule time to talk with them.*

Website connections *List all the on-line cross market strategies. The sewing company website might love to display your book and buy link. Same with the paranormal research websites. Try approaching the historical websites and asking to post my book there. Remember to give something back. Some websites will charge for an ad, others might love it if the author writes a brief blog occasionally that connects their site with my book.*

Guest blogging   *Strategize with blogs that are talking to my book's unique hooks and cross markets and offer to do a guest blog – not a blog about my book, a blog about what interests the blog reader with a secondary note that I am the author of a book that features history or historic clothing or lighthouses or whatever subject is appropriate.*

NOTE: Never just use the same content, each blog audience deserves a special approach.

Charities   *Approach appropriate charities, for example lighthouses are always trying to raise money, there might be a fund for retired historians or seamstresses. Possibly develop support for paranormal investigators. Find the most powerful charity to connect with my book and commit a portion of the book sales to that charity, or create a fundraising event for it.*

SCHEDULE

Cross Market 1	*Fashion*
Strategy	*Try to post on fashion websites*
Start Date	*June 1*
End Date	*June 30*
Test Tool	*Offer free book contest to followers of that website*
Evaluation	*Non-effective, no sales and no one tried to win free book*

Cross Market 2	*Historic*
Strategy	*Historic book clubs, lighthouse blogs and gift shops, historic clothing shop websites*
Start Date	*June 1*
End Date	*June 30*
Test Tool	*Interaction from this cross market*
Evaluation	*Many comments on blogs, good reception from book clubs,*

*some comments on posts at historic clothing shop
websites and gift shops at lighthouses. Unclear on
number of sales for this cross market, but worthy of
continued effort*

Cross Market 3	*Charity – raising funds for lighthouse upkeep*
Strategy	*Offering and gaining free promotions from charity, press campaign that book is raising funds for charity*
Start Date	*June 1*
End Date	*June 30*
Test Tool	*Sales through coded purchases (purchase only at one location or on-line book store for charity to receive funds)*
Evaluation	*Sales have shown very successful, continue for 6 more months.*

PLATFORM EXPANDING WORKSHEET

Looking at your SUPER Genres, you can now determine what platform venues you might like to approach. Develop a worksheet for yourself that lists each cross marketing direction then beneath each direction, all the possible venues you can find and research. It might look something like this:

- SUPER Genre direction: Scuba diving
  - Venue 1 – Scuba diving website #1 through #4
  - Venue 2 – Scuba diving stores, local, #1 through #4
  - Venue 3 – Scuba diving clubs, #1 through #4
  - Venue 4 – Scuba diving event at travel show, convention center

Once you have all the venues, their contact information, the contact name and noted whether they've ever done anything like this before, you can move on to developing a proposal worksheet for enticing them all.

CROSS MARKET PROPOSALS WORKSHEET

Now you must be creative. Before you even contact one of the people at any of these venues, you must have a plan for what you'd like to propose. I strongly suggest you develop twice as many ideas as you have venues, this way you have something to work with should they not like the first idea you propose. Make your proposals simple and clear; know what you are offering and what you want in return. Never forget, this must be a win/win opportunity for both you and the venue.

You will need to keep track of all your ideas, how long they will take for you to implement, and at what point you might be willing to walk away from a venue during the proposal process. Keep your idea lists under each venue category and carefully choose which one you want to propose to each venue. Do not make proposals to all your venues at once, start with one venue, either strike an agreement that the idea will work and begin soon, or walk away because you feel the venue isn't going to work for you.

There are four venues listed on your platform expansion worksheet and four directions to go under each venue. Choose one venue, explore and develop proposals for all four directions under it, then move on to the next.

Be sure to create proposals that are appropriate for each venue. For example, a store location might be a great place for a one time book signing, but not such a great place for a monthly event. Scuba clubs might be perfect for simple interaction, but not so great for setting up live chats or book promotions. On-line websites are different from bloggers who talk about diving. They both have a following perfect for your book, but each following must be approached differently.

After you've created all your ideas and all your directions within each venue, you should list them carefully so that you can shift those ideas around when necessary, expand upon them, or eliminate them altogether.

Write your proposals and keep them coded by number so that you know who has heard which proposal. Note which ones were rejected but still useable elsewhere, and which ones are accepted.

At this point I always begin an Excel spreadsheet to keep track of what I'm doing with each venue, when and with which element (blog, column, article, tip of the month, etc.)

CROSS MARKET MAINTENANCE WORKSHEET

This worksheet is simple but vital. It records your contact at each venue, all his/her contact information, which activity you are doing for them, when you started, and how your sales are growing since it began.

Maintaining your cross markets is all about being aware of everything going on with them. Does the business close on Christmas week? Do they sponsor an international scuba event once a year? Are they affiliated with a travel agent that sets up scuba group trips? Are they growing or are they having trouble keeping business? Who is their competition and what do they do?

Keeping good records helps you be ahead of the game. After your first year with them, you might discover that your sales have grown greatly because of your cross marketing efforts there. It might be time to inquire about being part of their international scuba event, or how you can connect with the travel agency to help sell books too.

Keep an eye on your involvement. Sometimes you might want to charge things up to spark more interest in your monthly column, or you might want to begin to back away and move on to a different venue.

Being completely on top of your cross marketing activities will help you know what is best for you and the venue. It will help you see the road ahead.

CROSS MARKETING EVALUATION WORKSHEET

The most important part of cross marketing is evaluating everything carefully. It will seem difficult at first. If a venue only brings in a 5% increase in book sales, when another venue brings in nearly 200% in the first quarter, it seems natural to simply eliminate the small seller. But is it smart? Always remember that you are cross marketing and these are venues no other author is approaching to sell their books. These are sales you would not otherwise have. They are also audiences you'd never be talking to if you subscribed to the author centipede mentality.

You must evaluate everything you do with these venues and only you can determine if it's worth your time and energy. If the venue that is only bringing in 5% per quarter continues to grow, it's a major success and is exposing you and your book to a new, broader audience.

But, there's always a chance that after two quarters, the fantastic venue bringing in a 200% sales jump simply falls flat. It could mean that you've penetrated this particular venue and there are no more books to sell there. Or it could mean that you got lazy, rode high on your success, and forgot to put the punch into your monthly article.

Evaluate deeply and honestly and record everything.

CROSS MARKETING EVALUATION WORKSHEET

First Quarter

- Venue #1 contact info – Mike Jones, email address, phone number
- Venue #1 project - Monthly weather adventure article
- Venue #1 time spent – 90 minutes per month for article writing and 2 hours per month promoting through my social networks and responding to comments
- Venue #1 notes – Mike wants to discuss a few new ideas
- Venue #1 book sales – 20% rise in book sales, spike with each monthly column entry

- Venue #2 contact info – Annie Smith, email address, phone number
- Venue #2 project - Monthly guest blog about diving around the world
- Venue #2 time spent – 40 minutes per month for blog writing and 1 hour per month promoting through my social networks and responding to comments
- Venue #2 notes – This blog has a TON of comments and very exciting following. I might like to propose more of these with other bloggers, but make sure Annie is happy with everything I'm doing on her blog.
- Venue #2 book sales – 40% rise in book sales, spike with each monthly column entry

- Venue #3 contact info – Joe McDonald, email address, phone number
- Venue #3 project - Monthly scuba tip
- Venue #3 time spent – 15 minutes per month for article writing and 1 hours per month promoting through my social networks and responding to comments
- Venue #3 notes – VERY FEW COMMENTS
- Venue #3 book sales – 5% rise in book sales, spike with each monthly column entry

How would you evaluate these three venues? Should one be eliminated? Should they all get a little more attention? Should you do more to promote your activities? Should venue #3 be reevaluated and possibly restructured with a different activity? How can you make venue #2, the surprise sales king, even better?

Evaluation is all about knowing all the facts and being flexible. Your cross marketing evaluation sheet should be loaded with impressions, thoughts and ideas to help you work through problems or make tough decisions.

PART 9
IN CLOSING

"Cock your hat – angles are attitudes."

~ Frank Sinatra

Writers are magicians of the highest order. Writers create something from nothing. They use the craft of illusion and emotion and generate mystical rhythms with words. They take us on journeys through time and place, other worlds, our own world, inner reality, and super reality. They take our hands and walk us through their imaginations, much the same way an artist or musician, scientist, dreamer, or even a rambunctious toddler in the park does. It's nothing short of extraordinary. And it takes more courage than most people know.

Rejection is a way of life for authors. The struggle to reach heights of visibility can be daunting. Critics, jealousy, industry practices, and insecurity can play havoc with an author's efforts. It's as difficult to become a rock star or movie star as it is to become a known author. But the reality is that every artist must find their own path to success. The author's bravery is amazing. They've put their heart and soul on paper and handed it to you. If that's not more terrifying than facing a fire breathing dragon, I can't imagine what is.

There's a passion and deep commitment inside each writer that compels them to put their story into words, tighten the plot, stretch the characters as far as possible, and polish it to a pristine shine. Whether fiction or nonfiction, every word is labored over with love and obsession. The efforts are extraordinary, especially considering the fact that writers live rather ordinary, busy, task filled lives like everyone else.

There's magic in the process of writing a book, but the magic required to market that book requires a little coaching. History has taught authors wrongly that their publishers will market and promote them. Not so. Not anymore. And with a crumbling and changing industry under their feet, authors must gird their loins for battle once more. It's time to call on all the enchantment a marketing wizard can muster.

I've heard it all. Authors have told me that they were raised to never boast. Get over it. They've explained that they feel like used car salesmen when they promote their books. They're promoting incorrectly. They've complained that there's no time to market, they would rather write. Why write the next book when no one has purchased their first one? The excuses mount up and become laughable. They don't believe in marketing. I don't believe in dieting but I'm still on a diet. They don't enjoy people. This one's a real problem, because people buy and read books. They hate Twitter, hate Facebook, refuse to blog, and see no sense in social networking. They are seeking the passive tools. The easy way. The short cuts.

There are no short cuts to success, ask anyone who's made it. It takes a lot of work and commitment to become successful no matter what you do. That's a fact. But there's good news.

Here's the real magic in creating sales success for authors – AUTHORS ARE ALREADY HIGHLY CREATIVE CREATURES! It takes a great amount of inventiveness to break barriers and forge a path to big book sales. Authors have that in spades! When I look at authors, whether I'm speaking, teaching a workshop, or working one-on-one with a coaching client, I can't help but be in awe of the vast amount of originality each writer has. Over the years, I've worked with people from all kinds of businesses. I once had a group of funeral homes as a marketing client. Creativity isn't the name of the game for clients like that. Working with authors is a joy in comparison. Except for one thing.

Most authors seem to forget how creative they are the moment the words marketing, promotions, or publicity come into the conversation. They shudder and become terrified rabbits. The most difficult job I have is reminding a writer how inventive, logical, and imaginative they are, and that it's not only okay, but important to use it for their marketing. Marketing, promotions, and publicity aren't foreign countries to be looked at from afar. There are no borders barring an author's unique solutions. In fact, the rules for marketing, promotions, and publicity are far more flexible than the rules for having a good book published. There's tons of opportunity for the wonderful concepts an author's mind might conjure. The basic rules for marketing, promotions, and publicity are simpler than the parameters for good writing, plotting, and editing.

If a writer understands that their creativity extends beyond the launch date of their book, everything changes. The author centipede mentality will dissolve and the author will be reaching out to more prospective fans and book buyers than ever before. With so many ways to buy and read a book these days, and so many readers out there hungry for good books, the sky's the limit for author success. The magic comes in not losing the magic. Never, for a single moment, imagine that your creativity isn't the key to everything, especially book sales success.

Writing the book is only half the journey. Using all the enchanting and mystical ingenuity that went into that book is the power that will pull you to sales success. *Cross Marketing Magic for Authors* is a guide to keeping your magic alive!

8 MAGIC SPELLS FOR SUCCESSFUL CROSS MARKETING:
A Quick Reference Cross Marketing Magic Handbook

"Conformity is the jailer of freedom and the enemy of growth."

~ John F. Kennedy

MARKETING AUTHORS NEED TO BUILD A BETTER MOUSETRAP

We all know the rigors of being an author. We have to plot the story, develop the characters, write the book, and find publication. That's the fun part. Now, thanks to drastic shifts in the publishing industry, we also have to market, promote, and publicize the book. Scary stuff, especially for the unique race of creative souls called writers. We just don't have it in our reclusive DNA to go so far, but what choice do we have?

There are wonderful ideas everywhere, books on basic marketing and promotion skills, workshops on platform building, and every producer of the dreaded author promotions is lurking inside our computer screen ready and willing to help us out. With just a few clicks of a cursor you too can have lovely imprinted mugs or fancy book videos. You may need these things, you may want these things, but oh, how confusing it all can get.

And there's the big question. Does this stuff work? We network with other authors who do contests and giveaways. Do those work? We even imitate some of the strategies we see, but are those strategies actually creating book sales?

The truth of the matter is that without book sales, real author success is out of reach. It's all good, every technique, every promotion, every contest. It's all very important too, because you must be visible and active, but if you are still not getting the results you want, what can an author do?

Simple. It's time to build a better mouse trap. To do that you need better materials, you need to place your trap in better locations and you must seed it with better cheese. In this case, magical cheese.

Promotion is important but have you looked carefully at how you create your promotions? Are they based on the success stories and events of other authors, or are they based on what's inside your manuscript? For example, if you're giving away a free book on Facebook, so is every other author with a Facebook account. But if your main character is a gardener suspected of murdering the dead man found beneath her petunias, and you promote your book to on-line gardening groups and communities in addition to your Facebook friends and fans, now you've expanded your reach in a big way!

Think about this. There are hundreds of gardening groups and communities on Facebook, Twitter, and Yahoo! all over the internet. There are more in your real life communities. Imagine one little tweak to your promotions that includes this entire new audience and what it can do for you. Look at all the new fans you'll meet in new places where you can introduce your book and offer book giveaways, whether on-line or in live speaking engagements.

This small adjustment can easily represent hundreds of sales for you, and all because you did what all the other authors do, but did it with a broader, more magical and unique brush stroke. You made sales from the marketing magic right inside your manuscript. Your promotions are now personal, powerful, and part of a much, much better mouse trap.

What's inside your manuscript that can make your marketing, promotions, and publicity seriously stand apart, and where can you find new targets for your strategies?

What follows are 8 magic spells to help you master and implement cross marketing so that it works miracles for your bottom line.

MAGIC SPELL 1 – Perfect the Basics

If you want to wash your clothes, you need to know the basics of how to do that. Long ago, it meant shaving bars of soap into hot water and rubbing your clothing across a washboard. These days, it's a little easier. You need a washing machine and detergent. Still, the basics are the basics and you need water, soap, and a vehicle to agitate the clothing and draw out the dirt.

- The basics for selling books are:
- A strong 25 word pitch

- Great author and book platforms
- Marketing
- Publicity
- Promotions

If you don't understand or use these basic tools correctly, you will find it much harder to create sales success.

A Strong 25 Word Pitch – You need a powerful 25 word pitch for each book, and if you have written a series, it's good to create a 25 word pitch for that series too. Within that 25 word pitch you must have the following information:

- Who will relate to your book? (The target demographic)
- What is the genre of your book? (If nonfiction, the specific subject and reader interest)
- What is your book about?

A good example of a 25 word pitch is: *Desperate to escape her tortured past, a teenage genius learns she has multiple personality disorder when she is arrested for the kidnapping and murder of her four-year-old half sister.* This pitch works because, without telling me this is a YA, I can easily identify the target reader through the description. The description also clearly tells me it is contemporary, and I know this story is powerful because the author held back no punches by telling us the kick to the story. Use your story description to tell the reader the genre and target the reader and your 25 word pitch will be successful.

This 25 word pitch will serve you for queries to literary agents, publishers, or reviewers. It is the power in your request letters for event participation or to schedule a book signing event of your own. It will be the biggest punch for your promotions, advertisements, tweets, and Facebook posts. It will be the meat of your press releases and the core for your publicity campaigns. Memorize your 25 word pitch, be able to spit it out at a moment's notice, and use it consistently everywhere you are, including and especially as part of your email signature. Your 25 word pitch will carry you a long way.

Great Author and Book Platforms – Whether you write fiction or nonfiction, you must have an author platform and a book platform. Platforms are the place from which you tell your whole story. You might tweet, or post on Facebook or a blog, but without a platform website for either your author image or your book information, you've got little to tweet or post or even blog about. Twitter, Facebook, and blogs are a vehicle to send fans and prospective book buyers to your platform websites where all your strength lies.

Author Platform - Your author platform is your business office. It is a subtle website, or blog with tabs that represents you as an author. It is designed to serve people wishing to know more about you. Those people include the media, book reviewers, local newspaper, on-line interviewers and publications, and prospective book buyers curious to see everything you have written beyond the books they already know about. Your author platform must always be kept current and up to date. You never know when the media might come calling. In this website you will have the following:

- Introduction/ home page – simple introduction and welcome
- Book(s) page – listing all your books and buy links
- Activities page – listing all your events and activities
- Media room – all downloadable items for the media to use
  - Author photo
  - Author bio
  - Jpeg of your book cover(s)
  - Brief synopsis of the book(s)
  - Copies of all the press releases you've sent out
  - All contact information

Book Platform – Your book platform website is your store front. This platform is designed to attract your fans and prospective book buyers and hold their interest. Like your author platform website, this one must be kept current, active, and interesting for the fan. This platform should be vibrant and entertaining with elements that bring your fans back again and again. Be creative here but also, be careful. Each book platform should be specific to genre. In other words, if you write romance, all of your romance books, no matter the subgenre, can reside on the same website.

A word of caution - if you write contemporary mainstream or subgenre romance, be very careful about intertwining your erotic romance on the pages with these books. Erotic works should be clearly identified and on their own page. And, if one of your subgenres happens to be YA romance, put your erotic romance on a completely different website.

Always respect and be aware of the audience coming to your website. People looking for your nonfiction are not interested in your genre fiction, so   nonfiction should have its own website. People seeking mysteries are not interested in your science fiction books, so keep those on separate websites. Target your websites to the primary reader at all times and you will sell more books.

Blogs and Blogging – Blogs and blogging are a major part of your platforms because they work as a vehicle to drive people toward your websites and your books.

I have a few words of warning about blogging. Never blog about writing, no one except other writers cares about the subject. Never blog on other author's blogs, they are your competition and their blog followers are more interested in them than you. Never blog unless your topics directly connect with the unique hooks in your book, and in turn connect with readers interested in those unique hooks. Gardeners love blogs about gardening. If your mystery's main character is a gardener and you blog about gardening and how it is part of your story, you will have pulled in a new audience. Most authors target genre readers and forget that book buyers do a lot of things in their everyday lives. Reach these book buyers through your unique story hooks. This sets you apart from all the other authors shouting for the genre lovers' attention.

Regarding guest blogging, don't do it on another author's blog and never do it on other authors' blogs for a book launch blog tour. It will not be effective because you are talking to another author's fans, not yours. If another author asks you to guest blog, they are usually just asking for a favor so that they won't have to blog that week. Kindly pass on the opportunity and protect your writing time. Instead, look for blogs that relate to your unique story hooks. Ask to guest blog on a gardening blog owned by an avid gardener. In fact, seek out several of these gardening bloggers and set up your own very effective book launch blog tour with them. That will be far more effective than shouting to some other author's fans to buy your book.

Social Networking – Under the category of platforms, are all your social networks including Twitter, Facebook, Yahoo! Groups, LinkedIn, Goodreads, and street teams. Be sure to always spend your social network time talking to, relating to, and interacting with prospective book buyers and fans. Step away from other authors.

Your ratios for Twitter and Facebook followers and friends should be 1 author for every 10 prospective book buyers or fans.

Locate Yahoo! Groups that speak to the unique hooks in your book and be an active member of those groups.

LinkedIn is fantastic for nonfiction, but there again, don't connect with other authors, connect with prospective book buyers. If your nonfiction is about managing money, be sure to connect with financial people, educators, and business people. If it's about organizing offices, connect with all kinds of businesses including horses and daycare facility managers.

Goodreads can work if you are willing to shout along with all your other author friends to genre lover groups. But if you're willing to get creative and develop your own group directly related to your unique story hooks, you could create a nice book sales growth.

Street teams are a slightly different form of social networking, because the author creates the street team from their existing fan base and encourages those fans to create awareness for the author and their book. It's kind of out of the author's hands at that point, but if you control the information fed to your street team, you can be sure of good results.

Marketing – What is marketing? Marketing is creating awareness for you and your book. Without marketing your promotions will fail, because seldom do people purchase something if they've never heard of it. Without effective marketing your publicity will fall on deaf ears because the media isn't interested in something they assume is unimportant because they've never heard of it either. Marketing is the backbone for everything.

Marketing is your 25 word pitch. It's your author platform and your book platform. It's your social networking and blogging. It's very important to market early and everywhere. Be consistent, be interesting, creative, and professional with your message. Use teasers to tantalize prospective book buyers and fans and get them excited about your coming book. Be targeted with your marketing and make sure everything you do and say speaks to someone who will buy your book. Be calculating with your time management, and pay attention to the responses you receive. One audience might be more responsive than another, and that will guide you when you're ready to use advanced marketing techniques for bigger sales.

Marketing is the most important basic skill for an author. Marketing is creating awareness. Never underestimate the power of awareness.

Publicity – What is publicity? Publicity is the use of the media to get your message out to the public. Publicity only works if you have news to impart. There are several ways to create news around your book. It could be as simple as announcing the release of the book, or it could be as complicated as creating an event around your book that will benefit a charity connected to your book's unique story hook.

Publicity starts with having a news story and works with a carefully organized and created press release contact list. If you choose to purchase a media contact list service, be aware that you will not own the list, only the service for usage of the list. If you chose to develop your own list, you will have control over maintaining it as well as building relationships with the media people on that list. It's hard work but very worth it.

A press release is nothing more than a query with a few tight rules. It will have no flourish of descriptions or elegant phrases. It must be news and nothing but hard, cold news. Who, what, where, why and when. Nothing more and nothing less. You must always include contact information at least twice in your press release and never forget, the core of that press release is your 25 word pitch.

Promotion – What is promotion? Promotion is the activity around which you sell your book. Promotion, like publicity, will not work without strong marketing to carry it.

Promotion will not work if your main following is other authors. Promotion will not work if you try to do it while standing in a crowd of other authors shouting out the same message, "Buy my book!"

Promotions should be created around your book's fan base and targeted to prospective book buyers interested in your book's unique hooks. Avoid the *100 Authors Romance Promotion* everyone's talking about. Stay away from the *50 Book Videos for the Mystery Lover* promos. Steer clear of any promotional concept that lumps several authors together in an effort to attract genre lovers into picking and choose. Stand alone with your promotions. Do them when others aren't doing them, and make sure they are targeted to your book buyers and no one else's.

MAGIC SPELL 2 – Locate Your Niche and Cross Markets

Standing apart is the key to success. Now that you know it's inefficient to huddle with other authors for your marketing efforts, it's time to make your own trail to success. Locating your niche markets and cross markets is far easier than you might think.

Niche marketing is all about finding unique, usually small but powerful target markets for your book. Looking closely at your book, your niche markets might include things like dog lovers, politics, fashion, or any number of underlying elements that drive your characters and plot. These are small markets that might work alone to create broader audiences, or might work in combination with your cross markets to create really strong prospective book buyer targets.

Cross marketing is a strategy designed to find more of your existing target markets in different ways and places than standard marketing. For example, if your book is romance, your target readers are women. The goal of cross marketing is to reach women in different ways and places than every other author is doing. What do women do and where do they do it?

Women belong to health clubs and biking clubs. They belong to professional clubs and organizations, like teachers groups, nursing groups, gardening clubs, and women's auxiliary clubs. They gather in places like beauty parlors and manicure shops, town meetings and hiking, camping, or swimming clubs. In other words, women are everywhere. Most authors will only approach their romance genre prospective book buyers through mediums related to the genre, like romance lovers book clubs and blogs. They forget that a woman who loves reading romance might very easily not belong to a romance readers' book club or even read romance blogs. She is living her life and stumbling onto her romance when seeking out a new book at the bookstore or on-line.

Identifying your cross markets and niche markets is the first step in expanding your communication with the book buying world, and your first step away from all those other yapping authors.

Once you've identified your niche and cross markets, all you need to do is locate them. What blogs are they reading? Where do they shop on-line? Where do they meet in the neighborhood? How can you connect with similar groups all over the country? On-line? Through websites like the kind that sell running shoes or vintage clothing or nail polish? What else do these niche and cross markets do? Does it relate to your book's unique story hooks? If so, you might have a possible, very profitable connection.

MAGIC SPELL 3 – SUPER Genre Gaming

Genres were created to help bookstores stock, display, and inventory books. Since then, the bookstores have created a real dilemma for authors by using their sales information to determine which books they will carry on their shelves and in turn, which books publishers will publish and which books and authors agents will represent. It's a real mess.

But when the book is being released or already on the market, genres take on a completely different use and meaning for the marketing author. Creative genre gaming changes everything we know about genres by opening whole worlds of possible book buyers for a book.

The basic genre game is all about looking inside your book to see how many different genres or subgenres you can add to your target marketing strategies. Is there romance in your mystery? You may be able to approach romance lovers to market your book. Is there a strong women's fiction audience for your YA book? That's a huge possibility, because sales statistics show that more women over fifty purchase YA books than young adults. The basic genre game helps authors find broader audiences through existing genres for their books.

SUPER Genre gaming is another thing altogether. Imagine the genre game on steroids. SUPER Genres can only be developed for one book at a time. They search out and identify any number of marketing targets and directions, and they are unique to only that book or series. This means two wonderful things for an author.

- You can see your expanded markets right in front of you and how they are connected to your book
- No other author can approach these targets because they are specific to your book, plot, and unique story hooks
- To develop your SUPER Genre, simply look deeply into your book and begin with an expanded genre like:
- Urban fantasy/ dog lovers *(because the main character is a veterinarian)*

The point of playing SUPER Genre gaming is to expand your thinking way beyond the cubbyhole accepted genre concepts. SUPER Genres can be as long as twenty words and expose a number of cross marketing, promotional, and publicity directions. For example, I pulled this SUPER Genre from a book I recently read:

- Urban fantasy/ paranormal/ werewolf/ vampires/ veterinarian/ animal health/ dog lovers/ natural foods/ survivalists/ ASPCA/ romance/ mountain living/ ancient gods/ politics/ magic/ supernatural/ ancient weapons

This SUPER Genre represents seventeen possible cross marketing directions for the author to use for targeting prospective book buyers. It has a possible charity for publicity, offers interesting niche markets, and uncovers several   ways in which to reach out to these audiences. All of these seventeen SUPER Genre elements may not work, but almost all of them are a completely new direction for an urban fantasy author to market.

MAGIC SPELL 4 – Develop Strategies

Obviously there many ways to reach out to the particular targets uncovered in your SUPER Genre list. Using just one element of the SUPER Genre – dog lovers – the first instinct is to reach out through your social networking. Search Twitter and Facebook for dogs and dog lovers and make friends and followers among them. After that, join Twitter and Facebook groups related to the subject of dogs and dog lovers. Now when you tweet and post on Facebook about dogs in an effort to reach out to dog lovers and tell them about your book, you know you'll be talking to the right audience.

Blogging is another strategy for reaching dog lovers. Start focusing your blog topics on dogs and how they relate to your story and book. Carefully choose your tags to optimize SEO. The next step is to locate dog lovers who blog about dogs and ask them if you may guest blog on their blog. Many of them would love to host an author for their followers to enjoy.

Groups are another way of strategically connecting with your dog lover audience. Be careful not to join a dog lovers' Yahoo! Group and just talk about your book. Instead, talk about dogs, be part of the discussions. Always have your book title, 25 word pitch, and buy link at the bottom of your emails.

Next, look into websites and businesses connected with dogs and dog lovers. Create unique ideas to pitch to them and choose which specific kinds of businesses you'd like to connect with. Think about the on-line businesses. Would you want to connect with a gourmet dog food and doggie treats company website? Find a few of them then develop ideas for a monthly article or pet question of the day.

Can you do a book signing at the local pet stores? Maybe set up a book launch tour that takes you from one pet store to another, and lets you play with the puppies while signing books or doing a reading.

How about doggie daycares? Would they be a good place to pitch a promotion? Perhaps one of them will let you write a monthly article in their customer newsletter. With all these articles, you will always talk about dogs then have a brief bio, your book title, and where it can be purchased at the end of the story.

How about the Animal Rescue League or the ASPCA? Can you help with a fundraising event, or better yet, create a fundraising event for them that will work beautifully as a publicity boost for you? You might even want to donate a portion of the proceeds from your book to your chosen charity. It's a nice thing to do, and good publicity too.

MAGIC SPELL 5 – Approaching Cross Markets

Now that you've located the live and on-line businesses and organizations you'd like to approach, it's important to do all the homework.

Research every business or organization. Who handles the company's website management? Who handles the company marketing? How do you contact them?

Examine each business's on-line presence. Is it a large business? Is the website active and changing regularly? Is it interactive? Do they have anything like the ideas you've created already on their website? Are they a business that is open to letting you speak to their customers?

Now you must create your proposals. Be sure each proposal is specific to that particular business or organization. You might want to develop several ideas so that if one is rejected, you have another in your pocket. These proposal ideas must be a win/win for both the business and you.

Make your proposals only to decision makers and be sure those proposals are loaded with enthusiasm and information. You must make sure the contact understands that what you propose to do – a monthly article, a monthly column on doggie talk, a monthly puppy tip, or a monthly game about doggie brains and how they work – will entertain and attract their customers.

Make sure the contact understands what you want in return, the opportunity to briefly promote your book at the end of each article.

These proposals can be made through email, on the telephone, or in person in the case of a local business. Strive to get face-to-face or at least ear to ear on the phone in all cases. Emails tend to lose impact.

MAGIC SPELL 6 – Maintaining Cross Markets

Once you get in the door, remember your commitment. Never miss a deadline, keep an open dialog with the contact to assure everyone is pleased with what you're doing. Keep your articles or involvement lively and interesting.

The goal is to have at least three different cross marketing venues active at one time. It's critical that you do three very different things one each of the three different venues. Everyone gets their own content and attention and that will keep each venue happy.

Naturally, through all this you will continue to build and grow your social networking targets for dog lovers, so every time you have an article go up on the gourmet doggie treats website, you will promote it on your Twitter and Facebook accounts. Every time your newest puppy tips column appears on the dog supplies website, you'll promote it. Each time you have a new puppy brains story on the growing healthy puppies website, you'll tell everyone.

You will also make note on your author and book platform websites that you are on these three company websites doing some cool things. You could even ask them for their logos to include on your websites. Occasionally you should even blog about your experiences with working with these three different companies.

All this promotion does three things for you.

- It promotes your activity to your fans and prospective book buyers
- It keeps your activities log lively and constantly changing, making you a vibrant, active author
- It brings customers to the companies as well as book sales to you

This is how you maintain your hard earned cross marketing venues.

MAGIC SPELL 7 – Expanding Cross Markets

Let's imagine you have been doing three cross market venue activities for nearly a year and for the most part, sales are really booming. These venues take little time and effort on your part, so you've decided to expand your cross marketing efforts and expose your book to even larger audiences.

You can either reach out to more dog supply businesses, or you can move on to a different element in your SUPER Genre list. Because mountain living and natural foods are on your SUPER Genre list and represent a large part of your plot and story, you might decide to get creative and move in that direction.

Locate all the on-line and live businesses that relate to natural food and mountain living.

That list might include:

- Whole food stores
- Specialty food stores
- Vegetarian restaurants
- Health food and nutrition stores
- Mountain resorts
- Log cabin builders
- Forestry preservation organizations
- National parks and recreation
- Craft businesses that use the name mountain living in their description

Any one of these might be a fantastic direction for cross marketing, but you know the drill. Do your homework. Research each company's on-line presence and determine if they are a viable venue for you to sell books and offer value to. Locate all the correct contacts, develop your proposals and make your win/win presentations. This can open the door for a whole new target for your book. Remember to build this new audience into your social networking and contact bloggers on the subject to gain even more exposure.

Expanding your cross markets means dedicating your energy to the development and nurturing of a new audience, so before you do anything, make sure it's a large enough target. If you choose to reach out to a cross market targeted to survivalists and then discover that there is very little web presence and very few businesses or organizations to approach, you should pass on the idea. It's also important for you to seriously consider the audience and whether these survivalists would be interested in your urban fantasy about a veterinarian and a werewolf.

One more note. Only expand your cross markets when you are ready and have the time to commit to the effort required. Always review your sales for each existing cross marketing effort before expanding. It may be time for a venue to go, or it might be time to determine that a venue costs you too much time and energy for the results. Expanding is all about reaching a higher and higher level of sales. Never expand unless you have a sales goal in mind.

MAGIC SPELL 8 – Determining Effectiveness

How do you know if a cross marketing effort or venue is working? How do you know if the turkey is cooked? How do you know if your clothes are clean or your car has enough gas to make it across town? You check often and test for results. A turkey is fully cooked at 165 degrees. Your clothes are clean if the dirt is gone. The car has enough gas if the meter shows it has as much it takes to get across town. The same concepts work for cross marketing effectiveness.

The first tool you need is your goals. If you expect a 15% growth in your sales from each cross marketing venue or effort, then you will know immediately that a 2% growth is ineffective, but a 30% growth is great. The way to test effectiveness is to use one of the following seven methods.

- **Test by Timing** – for this technique, you choose a day of the week or a week of the month and run your promotions on specific venues only during those periods. If venue #1 does really well during its time period, but venue #2 does not so well during its exclusive promotional period, you have a good idea of which venue is more effective.
- **Control Activity** – I know several authors who have used this technique to prove that what their author friends were doing was less effective than their cross market efforts. During a month when other authors were running the big free book giveaway, the cross marketing authors did something not only different, but in a far more controlled manner. They did a buy one get the second book free promo, and marketed the promotion to four different target cross markets during the week. The cross marketing authors sold more books, not just because their counterparts only did free giveaways, but because with every marketing effort, they were talking to a much broader audience. Even if they'd only given books away, they would have beaten the other authors by a mile. Why? The other authors were marketing to more authors and genre lovers groups, while the cross marketing authors had connected with audiences based on their unique hooks. Oh, and by the way, those unique story hook audiences heard no other authors shouting to give away books, only the cross marketing author's deal.
- **Contests and Giveaways** – You all know how these work. Be careful to regulate the audiences you're offering these promotions to. That way you'll be able to easily see which target audience responded best.
- **Test by Location** – This can be done by city or it can be done by social network location. Offer a promotion on Twitter but not Facebook for a whole month. Then make the same offer the next month on Facebook only. Which network brought the most sales? This will tell you which network needs more nurturing as well as a stronger target cross marketing connection. To test by city, you would activate your   street

team in a specific city and have them run a local promotion for your book. If Atlanta sells more books than Seattle but Pittsburgh sells more books that the other two cities combined, you will know several things: which city is more interested in your book, which city is more uniquely connected to the story hooks inside your book, and which city has a more efficient street team.

- **Code Words** – For this testing technique, you would create a promotion for one specific cross market target instructed to use a specific code word when responding, and do the same promotion for a completely different cross market target, and instruct them to use a different code word when responding. For example, the code word "Spot" might be used for your dog lovers cross market target, and the word "wheatgrass" would be used by your health food cross market target. Again, the results will tell you which target is more responsive.

- **Journaling** – Keeping a record of everything is another way to track promotion effectiveness and audience response. If you ran a promotion for a person to win a full collection of your book series to your dog lovers target market the same day a famous vet runs a similar promotion on his book about keeping a dog healthy, you will probably not do so well. Recording that experience will help you keep your ears perked for such a conflict next time you do a promotion.

- **Elimination** – If you're wondering if a venue, social network, promotional idea or specific cross market audience is working or responding, simply eliminate them for 30 days and see what happens to your sales. You will gain a lot of answers with this technique.

- **One Final Note on Testing** – Give a promotion or target cross market audience at least 90 days before testing or considering the elimination of the audience. It takes that long for people to catch on to what you're doing and respond. Be patient. Also, keep in mind, some results might be skewed simply because the promotion wasn't powerful enough or the incentive wasn't effective. You are also part of the experiment, so do your best to create interesting, exciting, and enticing promotions.

ABOUT THE AUTHOR

Deborah Riley-Magnus is an author and an Author Success Coach. She has a twenty-seven-year professional background in marketing, advertising, and public relations and has been a writer for print, television, and radio.

As an Author Success Coach she produces several pieces monthly for various websites and online publications. She teaches online and live workshops, clinics, and boot camps. She writes an author marketing industry blog and coaches authors, one-on-one, for sales success. Deborah belongs to several writing and professional organizations.

She has lived on both the east and west coast of the United States and has traveled the country widely. She is a native of Pittsburgh, Pennsylvania and recently returned after living in Los Angeles, California for several years.

Blog - http://rileymagnus.wordpress.com/
Teach - http://theauthorsuccesscoach.com/
Fiction – http://drmagnusfantasy.com/
Tweet – http://twitter.com/rileymagnus
Facebook - http://www.facebook.com/deborah.rileymagnus
LinkedIn - https://www.linkedin.com/profile/view?id=66062158&trk=nav_responsive_tab_profile

READING LIST

The Artist's Way; Julia Cameron

How to Write a Book Proposal; Michael Larsen

Guerilla Marketing for Writers; J. Conrad Levinson, Rick
Frishman and
Michael Larsen

Guerilla PR; Michael Levine

Guerilla Publicity; J. Conrad Levinson, Rick Frishman and Jill
Lublin

Positioning, The Battle for your Mind; Al Ries and Jack Trout

The Sell Your Novel Tool Kit; Elizabeth Lyon

*The Zen of Social Media Marketing: An easier way to build
credibility, generate buzz and increase revenue*; Shama Kabani
and Chris Brogan

Six Thinking Hats; Edward De Bono

*A portion of the sales of this book will be donated to the American
Literacy Council. The American Literacy Council's main purpose is to
convey information on new solutions, innovative technologies, and tools
for engaging more boldly in the battle for literacy.*

www.ingramcontent.com/pod-product-compliance
Lightning Source LLC
Chambersburg PA
CBHW080253180526
45167CB00006B/2515